Woodworking Projects for the Country Home

◆

Lavon B. Smith

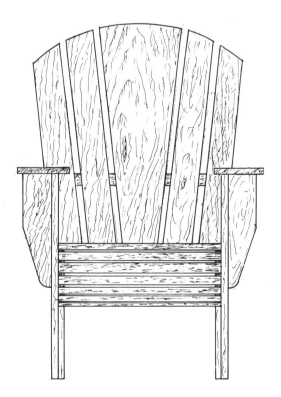

 Sterling Publishing Co., Inc.   New York

DEDICATION

To my three children, Jerry, and in memory of
Mary Lavon and Dwight.

L.B.S.

ACKNOWLEDGMENTS

Contributing Editors: Lawrice Brazel and
   Matthew Jones
Photography in color section courtesy of
   Creative Woodworks & Crafts
Material on stencilling provided by
   Zula Erickson
Marbleizing material and painting by
   Susan Stallman

Library of Congress Cataloging-in-Publication Data

Smith, Lavon Benson.
   Woodworking projects for the country home/by Lavon B. Smith.
      p.   cm.
   Includes index.
   ISBN 0-8069-8422-8
   1. Wooodwork.   2. House furnishings.   I. Title.
TT180.S498   1992
684'.08—dc20   91-41542
                                                     CIP

Edited by Rodman Pilgrim Neumann

10 9 8 7 6 5 4 3 2 1

Published in 1992 by Sterling Publishing Company, Inc.
387 Park Avenue South, New York, N.Y. 10016
© 1992 by Lavon B. Smith
Distributed in Canada by Sterling Publishing
 % Canadian Manda Group, P.O. Box 920, Station U
Toronto, Ontario, Canada M8Z 5P9
Distributed in Great Britain and Europe by Cassell PLC
Villiers House, 41/47 Strand, London WC2N 5JE, England
Distributed in Australia by Capricorn Link Ltd.
P.O. Box 665, Lane Cove, NSW 2066
Manufactured in the United States of America
All Rights reserved

Sterling ISBN 0-8069-8422-8

Contents

Color section follows page 64.

INTRODUCTION

Woodworking Projects for the Country Home assumes that you have some experience and familiarity with woodworking. However, the projects span a wide range of experience levels with many projects suitable for the beginner, and plenty of challenges for the more advanced woodworker.

The projects are specifically tailored for their use in or around the country home. The first section rounds out the theme of country home decor. A second section concentrates on objects that primarily require turning wood on a lathe. Display and decorative accessories are presented, followed by projects that are particularly suitable to the country kitchen. The last section includes outdoor pieces for the garden and patio as well as two handy projects to help out in your workshop.

Some of the projects, such as the Adirondack Chair, are similar to existing work; however, each project is the author's original creation in the details of its design and execution.

Each project includes a brief introduction, a photograph of the completed project, and then complete, detailed instructions with accompanying illustrations. You are led through the project in a step-by-step manner; nevertheless, it is always advisable to read everything through completely before starting any project.

SAFETY

While power tools may come to mind first when safety in the workshop is mentioned, there are many other hazards that cause more injuries in numbers, if not in severity. Shop maintenance, electricity, and hand tools can present safety hazards equal to power tools.

Some basic guidelines should be observed at all times.

- Provide proper lighting positioned so the area of operation is clearly visible.

- Do not operate machines while fatigued or drowsy.
- Protect eyes from dust and flying particles with a face shield or safety glasses that provide protection from the sides as well as the front.
- Wear a dust mask to avoid breathing in fine particles.
- As required, wear earmuffs to avoid permanent ear damage. Keeping blades sharp will also help to reduce noise.
- Avoid wearing loose clothing, rings and other jewelry. Wear shoes that have good traction and offer insulation from electrical shock. When handling lumber, wear gloves to prevent injury from splinters. Keep long hair tied back or otherwise secured to prevent its being tangled in moving machine parts.
- Clamp the work securely to the workbench, and use the guards provided with power equipment.
- Store paint, thinner, and other combustible materials in a separate storage area.

Hazardous shop maintenance is more than poor housekeeping, Floors cluttered with scrap wood, shavings, and other debris often lead to trouble. Power tools should not be used as tables for setting other tools and materials. Work surfaces should be kept clean and free of unnecessary items. Hand power tools and cords should be kept out of the way to protect the tool from being jerked from tabletop to floor, and the worker from tripping.

Keep the floors free of oil, water, or any other slippery substance. Water is especially hazardous when working around power tools. Machines should always be properly grounded. Simple shorts in motors, switches, or other wiring can convert ungrounded machines into lethal devices with your body as the electrical conductor from hot machine to ground.

Electrical circuits should have fuses or trip switches of specified amperages; overloading is the cause of many fires. Keep machines and cords in good repair, making sure that the third—or ground—prong on 110 volt plugs is intact and used. Double-insulated tools do not require the ground prong, but for other machines the ground prong might be the only ground wire.

Before changing blades or performing maintenance on machines, turn off the machine and unplug it. Check to make sure motor pulleys and belts are well covered. Turn machines off and allow them to come to a full stop before making adjustments. Keep blades sharp and properly secured.

Similarly, keep cutting edges of hand tools sharp, and check handles on files, chisels, hammers, and screwdrivers. When using cutting tools, cut away from your body to prevent injury in case the tool slips. Store hand tools so that the cutting edges are protected.

Lavon B. Smith

Country Home Decor

1 ◆ PICTURE FRAME

Here is a practical, decorative picture frame that makes a handsome present, suitable for a variety of picture framing purposes. You can surprise someone special with a beautiful gift or enhance your own home's decor with a custom frame and favorite picture. The frame itself is simple to make and its different approach to frame construction is designed to produce the tightest joints.

SUPPLIES

- Matt for an 11″ × 14″ picture to fit in a 16″ × 20″ frame
- Four 1½″ No. 8 sheetrock screws
- Four wood plugs cut from scrap parts
- Wood glue
- Twelve glazier's points
- Sawtooth hanger
- ¾″ plywood board
- "C" clamps
- Try square
- Tape measure
- Ruler/straightedge
- Transparent tape
- Glass cutter (optional)
- Mitre box (optional)
- Radial-arm saw, table saw, or other cutting tool
- Drill
- Drill bits: ⅛″ and ⅜″
- Screwdriver
- Belt sander (optional)
- Sandpaper in coarse and medium grit
- Router
- ⅜″ Roman ogee bit or ⅜″ rounding-over bit
- 000 steel wool
- Stain
- Clear satin polyurethane varnish

Materials	Quantity
Lumber, ⅞″ × 1⅝″, cut to 23″ length	2
Lumber, ⅞″ × 1⅝″, cut to 19″ length	2
Single-strength glass, 16″ × 20″	1
Heavy cardboard backing, 16″ × 20″	1

INSTRUCTIONS

This construction method, while only one of many ways to make a frame, has several advantages. For example, an unconventional feature is that none of the routing operations is performed until the frame has been assembled and sanded. This provides exactly fitted, mitred joints. Another advantage is that the use of screws makes a secure glue joint at the mitred corners. Plugs, cut from the same material as the frame and sanded flush, are used to cover screwheads and enhance the frame's appearance.

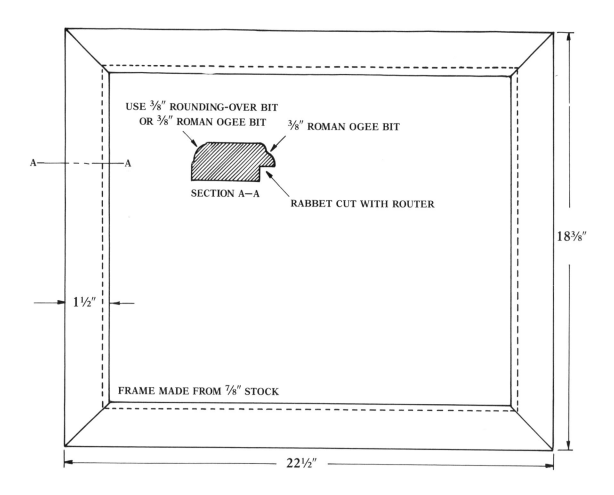

USE ⅜″ ROUNDING-OVER BIT
OR ⅜″ ROMAN OGEE BIT   ⅜″ ROMAN OGEE BIT

A———A

SECTION A—A

RABBET CUT WITH ROUTER

18⅜″

1½″

FRAME MADE FROM ⅞″ STOCK

22½″

Illus. 1.1   Assembly and dimensions of frame parts with cross section of frame.

Basic Cutting

Rip the frame material to width, allowing ⅛″ for smoothing edges on the jointer. Cut parts to rough length, leaving about 1″ extra for cutting the 45° mitres on each end (Illus. 1.1). Next, true up the two edges of each board on the jointer.

Set up for cutting a 45° angle on the radial-arm saw, table saw, mitre box, or other cutting tool. Make a test cut on a scrap board and check the 45° angle with a try square. After adjusting the saw, cut a 45° angle on one end of each board. Cut the 45° angle on the other end of each board making sure the two sides are exactly the same length and the two ends the same. A stop set up on the saw will assure accurately cut parts.

Assembly

Clamp a ¾″ plywood board on top of the work table, with the front and one end extending out over the table edge. The plywood board serves as a means of clamping the frame parts together with "C" clamps during assembly.

Lay one of the side boards of the frame along the front edge of the plywood and clamp securely in place with a "C" clamp. Place small strips of wood under the clamps to protect the frame. Apply glue to the 45° cut, then lay an end board of the frame on the plywood and fit the mitred cuts together to form a joint. Clamp the end board in place making sure the mitred joint is pressed together firmly (Illus. 1.2).

Bore a ⅜″ hole halfway through one of the boards at the joint. Drill a ⅛″ pilot hole

Illus. 1.2   Clamping mitre joint in place with "C" clamps.

Illus. 1.4   Gluing a plug in counterbored hole.

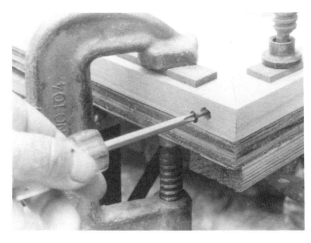

Illus. 1.3   Driving screw to secure the joint.

Illus. 1.5   Routing rabbet in back side of frame.

through the remaining half of the board. Drive a screw through the hole (Illus. 1.3) to draw the joint together and secure the two parts in place.

After all four corners are secure, glue a wood plug in each of the ⅜″ counterbored holes (Illus. 1.4), leaving enough of the plug extending from the hole to be sanded flush after the glue dries.

Routing

Sand all surfaces with coarse grit paper, followed by a sanding with medium grit. Turn the frame front side up and rout around both the inside and outside edges with a ⅜″ Roman ogee bit. Turn the frame over and rout a ⅜″

rabbet ¼″ deep around the inside edge to accommodate the glass, matt, and backing (Illus. 1.5).

Finishing

Fine-sand all surfaces. Apply stain and allow eight hours drying time. Apply three coats of clear satin polyurethane varnish (allow each coat to dry and hand rub with 000 steel wool before application of each coat).

Mounting and Framing

The exploded view (Illus. 1.6) shows how the picture, frame, and matt fit together when mounting and framing. The picture should be

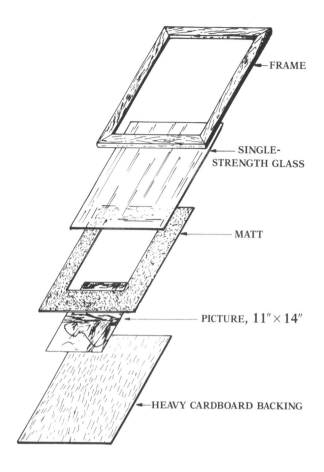

FRAME

SINGLE-STRENGTH GLASS

MATT

PICTURE, $11'' \times 14''$

HEAVY CARDBOARD BACKING

Illus. 1.6   Exploded view showing assembly of frame, glass, matt, picture, and backing.

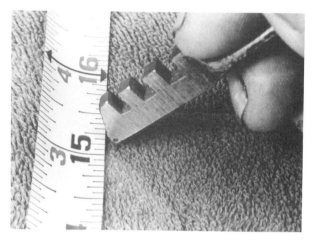

Illus. 1.7   Marking location of cut to be made across the glass with glass cutter.

Illus. 1.8   Cutting alongside straight edge connecting small cut marks on opposite sides of glass.

attached to the back side of the matt with transparent tape before assembly. The glass may be measured (Illus. 1.7) and cut to size with a straightedge and glass cutter (Illus. 1.8), or you may have a professional framer cut the glass. Glazier's points are used to secure all parts in place. Attach a saw-tooth hanger to the midpoint of the top on the back side of the frame.

2 ◆ HALL MIRROR

You may find in this hall mirror and coat rack the welcoming touch that is just right for your front hallway or by the back door. A small shelf with a drawer underneath serves well for keeping gloves and storing keys or loose change. Two decorative pegs at the bottom are for umbrellas. Coat and hat hangers similar to those pictured can be purchased at most hardware suppliers.

SUPPLIES

- Mirror glass, ¼″ × 11½″ × 15″
- Two decorative pegs, for umbrellas
- Two coat–hat hangers with screws
- Two ¾″ porcelain knobs
- Twenty-four 1¼″ No. 8 sheetrock screws
- ½ lb. Finish 4 penny nails
- Saw (hand and/or band saw, scroll saw, jigsaw)
- Drill
- Drill bits
- Dowelling jig
- Dowels
- Hammer
- Pipe clamps
- Wood glue
- Belt sander
- Sanding belts
- Sandpaper
- Router
- ⅜″ rounding-over bit
- ⅜″ Roman ogee bit
- Nail set
- Finishing sander
- "C" clamps
- Tack cloth
- Stain
- Polyurethane finish

INSTRUCTIONS

The front frame overlaps the opening in the back frame to allow the mirror to be installed through the back opening and up against the back side of the front frame. Both frames are of simple construction. Made with butt joints dowelled and glued, they require no special tools other than those available in most home workshops.

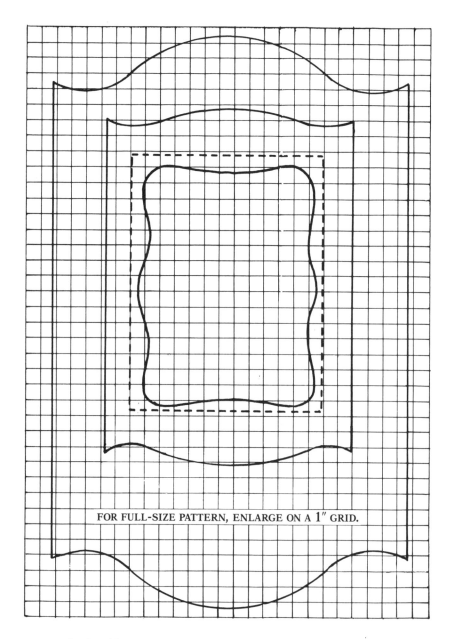

FOR FULL-SIZE PATTERN, ENLARGE ON A 1″ GRID.

Illus. 2.1 Pattern on one-inch grid.

Basic Cutting

Enlarge the patterns for parts having curved lines by using the grid method (Illus. 2.1). Cut all parts to size, then drill dowel holes in the frame parts at the indicated locations (Illus. 2.2 and 2.3). Dowel and glue the frame parts together (Illus. 2.4, 2.5, and 2.6), then clamp in place with pipe clamps until the glue dries (Illus. 2.7).

Sand front and back of each frame with a belt sander. Transfer patterns to each frame and cut curved parts on each end with a band saw or other saw capable of cutting curved lines. The curves on the inside of the smaller frame can be cut out with a scroll saw or jigsaw. Sand all edges smooth.

Rout around outside of each frame along top edge with a ⅜″ rounding-over bit. Rout

Materials			Quantity
Larger frame pieces:	A	$\frac{3}{4}'' \times 13'' \times 24''$	1
	B	$\frac{3}{4}'' \times 7'' \times 24''$	1
	C	$\frac{3}{4}'' \times 5'' \times 19\frac{1}{2}''$	2
Smaller frame pieces:	D	$\frac{3}{4}'' \times 6'' \times 19\frac{1}{8}''$	1
	E	$\frac{3}{4}'' \times 4'' \times 19\frac{1}{8}''$	1
	F	$\frac{3}{4}'' \times 4'' \times 17''$	2
Shelf:		$\frac{3}{4}'' \times 5'' \times 13\frac{1}{2}''$	1
Drawer housing: end		$\frac{1}{2}'' \times 3\frac{1}{2}'' \times 4''$	2
top and bottom		$\frac{1}{2}'' \times 3\frac{1}{2}'' \times 11''$	2
Drawer box: end		$\frac{1}{2}'' \times 2\frac{1}{2}'' \times 3\frac{1}{2}''$	2
front and back		$\frac{1}{2}'' \times 2\frac{1}{2}'' \times 10''$	2
Drawer front:		$\frac{1}{2}'' \times 3'' \times 11''$	1
Plywood mirror backing:		$\frac{1}{4}''$ thick, cut to fit	1

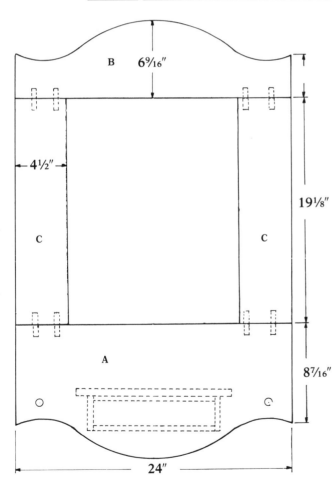

Illus. 2.2 Layout of frame pieces with dotted lines indicating dowel pin locations and position of drawer–shelf assembly.

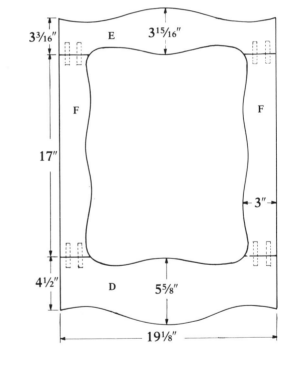

around the inside of the smaller frame with a $\frac{3}{8}''$ Roman ogee bit. Rout the front and end edges of the small shelf with a $\frac{3}{8}''$ rounding-over bit. Finish sand all parts, first with medium grit (100–150) garnet paper followed with fine grit (180–220) garnet paper.

Illus. 2.3   Drilling hole in frame piece for dowel.

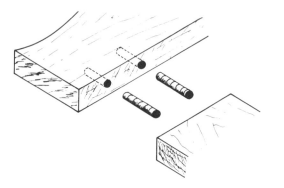

Illus. 2.4   Dowelling and gluing frames.

Illus. 2.6   Assembling dowelled frame pieces.

Illus. 2.5   Gluing dowels.

Illus. 2.7   Using pipe clamps to keep dowel joints tight as the glue dries.

Shelf and Drawer Housing Assembly

After all parts of the shelf and drawer housing are sanded, assemble the drawer housing (Illus. 2.8). The top and bottom are fitted between the two ends with butt joints. Apply a small amount of glue to each joint, then fasten by driving No. 4 finishing nails through previously drilled pilot holes in end pieces. Set the nail heads below the wood surface with a nail set. After glue dries, sand all surfaces flush with a finishing sander.

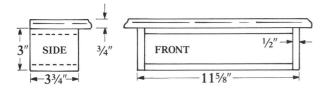

Illus. 2.8 Shelf and drawer housing assembly.

Glue the shelf to the top of the drawer housing and clamp in place with "C" clamps. The back edge of the shelf should be flush with the drawer housing in order to allow the assembly to be mounted flat against the frame surface.

Drawer Assembly

Drawer parts are attached with butt joints secured with glue and No. 4 finishing nails in much the same manner as the drawer housing.

First, fasten the back and front boards to the bottom with glue and nails (Illus. 2.9). Fasten end pieces as shown in the plans. Sand joints flush after the glue dries.

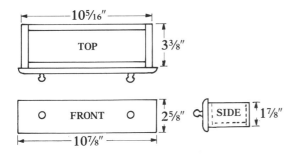

Illus. 2.9 Drawer assembly.

The drawer front is made to overlap the drawer box ¼" all around. Rout around front edges of the drawer front with a ¼" rounding-over bit. Attach the drawer front to drawer box with glue and secure in place with "C" clamps until the glue dries. Sand the drawer front with 220 grit garnet paper. Drill holes for the knobs.

Frame Assembly

Place the larger frame face side up on a flat surface. Arrange the smaller frame and the drawer and shelf housing in place on the larger frame, then mark around the outside with a pencil. Remove the frame and housing. Mark the location of screw holes inside the marked area. Drill a ⅛" hole through the frame at each mark. Turn the frame over and countersink the holes from the back side.

Finishing

Clean dust from all parts and apply stain. Allow the stain to dry. Using the pencil marks as a guide, arrange front frame in place and secure it to back frame by driving 1¼" No. 8 screws from the back side of the larger frame. Attach the shelf and drawer housing in the same manner. Drill holes for the umbrella pegs and secure them in place with glue (Illus. 2.10). Apply polyurethane finish in three thin coats allowing each to dry before applying the next. Sand lightly between coats with 220 grit garnet paper.

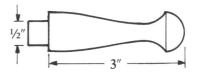

Illus. 2.10 Umbrella peg. Available at most lumber and hardware suppliers.

Attach the hat–coat rack hangers on each side of the mirror with the screws provided.

Installing the Mirror

Install mirror from back side and secure in place with a ¼" plywood backing.

3 ◆ MAGAZINE RACK

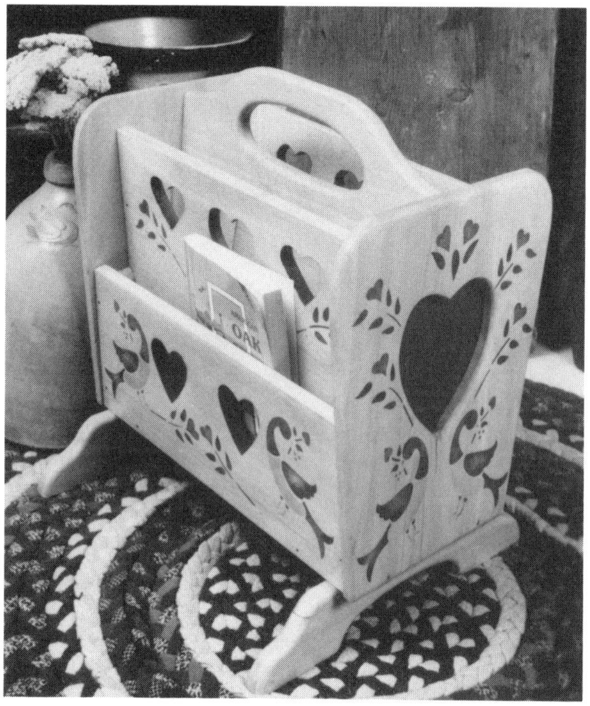

The cutout hearts and folk stencilling of this useful piece will add a distinctive warmth to your country home decor. Two separate assemblies, an inside and an outside rack, are constructed and then combined to form this good-looking magazine rack. There is a convenient handle and plenty of room for your favorite magazines.

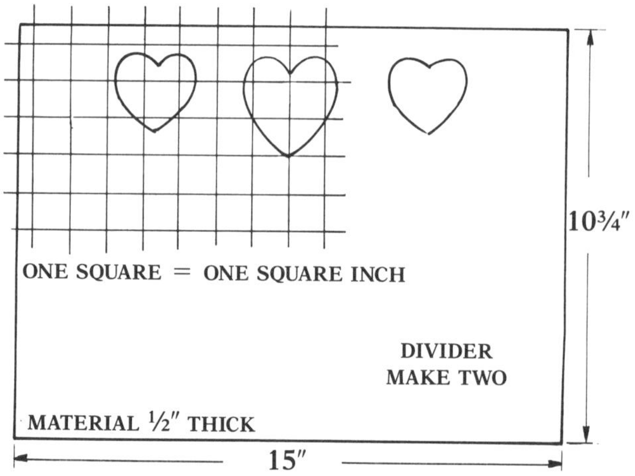

ONE SQUARE = ONE SQUARE INCH
DIVIDER
MAKE TWO
MATERIAL ½″ THICK
15″
10¾″

Illus. 3.1 Divider. For full-size pattern, enlarge on one-inch grid.

Materials		Quantity
Divider	½″ × 15″ × 10¼″	2
Inside end	½″ × 9½″ × 7″	2
Side	½″ × 15″ × 6¼″	2
End	½″ × 11¾″ × 13″	2
Bottom	¾″ × 15″ × 6¾″	1
Feet	¾″ × 14¾″ × 2½″	2
Handle	¾″ × 15″ × 5″	1

SUPPLIES

- Scroll saw
- Router
- ¼″ rounding-over bit
- 1¾″ No. 8 flat head wood screws
- 1½″ panelling nails, to match color of stained wood
- Sandpaper, 80–120 grit, 150–220 grit
- Stain
- Stencilling kit or similar supplies
- Polyurethane varnish

INSTRUCTIONS

The first step is to transfer the patterns to the wood. The layout for each piece that has a curved line to be cut—such as the divider (Illus. 3.1)—is reproduced at a reduced size on a grid pattern that was originally one inch by one inch. To reproduce the full-size pattern simply use a mechanical means (pantograph) or a machine (photocopier) to enlarge by the proper amount.

Basic Cutting

Enlarge the patterns for the inside rack assembly (Illus. 3.1, 3.2). Similarly, enlarge the patterns for the outside rack assembly (Illus. 3.3, 3.4, 3.5, 3.6, 3.7).

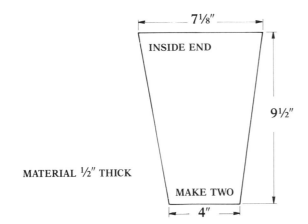

Illus. 3.2   Inside end. Follow dimensions for layout.

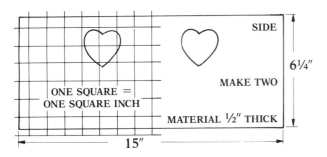

Illus. 3.3   Side. For full-size pattern, enlarge on one-inch grid.

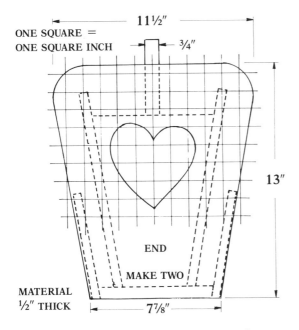

Illus. 3.4   End. For full-size pattern, enlarge on one-inch grid.

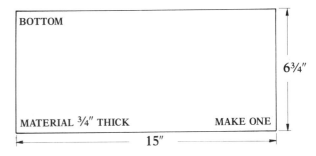

Illus. 3.5   Bottom. Follow dimensions for layout.

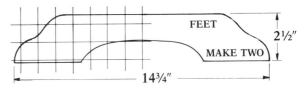

Illus. 3.6   Feet. For full-size pattern, enlarge on one-inch grid.

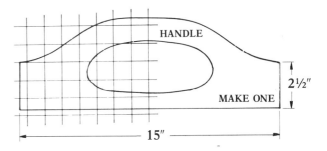

Illus. 3.7   Handle. For full-size pattern, enlarge on one-inch grid.

Transfer these patterns to the wood and cut the wood parts to shape. Use a scroll saw to cut the heart designs and the handle cutout.

Sand all the parts, including edges, with medium-grit garnet paper (80 to 120 grit). Rout around the edges that will be exposed using a ¼″ rounding-over bit. Fine-sand all parts using 150 to 220 grit garnet paper.

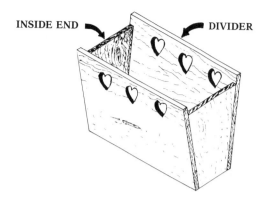

Illus. 3.8   Inside rack assembly.

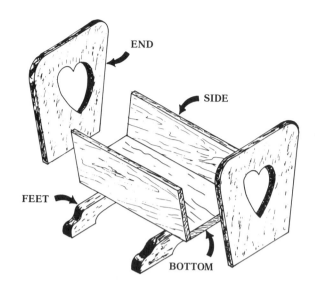

Illus. 3.9   Outside rack assembly.

Assembly

Assemble the dividers and inside ends to form the inside rack (Illus. 3.8). Assemble the sides, ends, and bottom to form the outside rack (Illus. 3.9). Secure the feet to the bottom with screws. Also secure the inside rack at either end between the outside rack. Attach the handle between the ends.

Finishing

Fine-sand as needed and apply stain. Make sure the piece is thoroughly dry before stencilling, and again before applying protective coats of varnish. If this is your first stencilling project, you may want to start with any of the very fine stencil kits that are readily available. The preparation of the paint and brushes is as important as the handling of the stencil plates and brush technique. Working carefully through the instructions with a kit may be your best approach.

4 ◆ OAK DESK

Made of oak or walnut, this desk is functional for home or office. The solid hardwood top, full extension file drawer, and five additional drawers provide ample storage and work space.

SUPPLIES

- Table saw
- Jointer
- Glue
- Clamps
- Sandpaper, 100, 120, and 180 grit
- Router, ⅜″ rounding-over bit
- Yellow glue, ½ pint
- 100 dowel pins, ⅜″ × 1½″
- 100 screws, 1¼″ No. 8
- 6 drawer pulls
- Brads
- Drill
- Stain
- Finish of your choice
- 5 pairs of drawer guides, 22″ side mount
- 1 pair of drawer guides. 20″ side mount

INSTRUCTIONS

The construction of this handsome desk is made easier by using a panel-making method that requires only those tools found in most home workshops. Panel frames are the basis of the desk foundation (Illus. 4.1), forming the back and the left and right drawer chests, which are joined by the middle drawer chest and fronted by a frame facing.

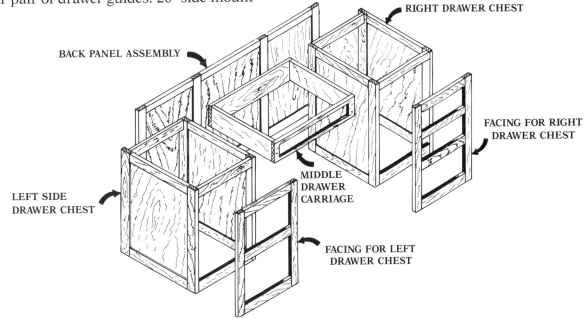

Illus. 4.1   Exploded view of panel frame and desk foundation assembly.

Materials			Quantity
Basic lumber:	Oak	$13/16'' \times 2'' \times 28''$	12
		$13/16'' \times 2'' \times 18''$	7
		$13/16'' \times 5\frac{1}{2}'' \times 27''$	1
		$13/16'' \times 2'' \times 20''$	14
		$13/16'' \times 2'' \times 28''$	2
		$\frac{1}{4}'' \times 24'' \times 28''$	6
	Oak plywood	$\frac{1}{4}'' \times 28'' \times 28''$	1
Desk top:	Oak	Total: $13/16'' \times 27'' \times 67''$	—
	Oak strips	$\frac{1}{2}'' \times 1'' \times 67''$	2
		$\frac{1}{2}'' \times 1'' \times 24''$	2
Desk drawers:	Plywood	$\frac{1}{4}'' \times 12\frac{7}{8}'' \times 21\frac{1}{8}''$	5
		$\frac{1}{4}'' \times 19\frac{1}{8}'' \times 20\frac{3}{8}''$	1
	No. 3 white pine	$\frac{3}{4}'' \times 9'' \times 12''$	2
		$\frac{3}{4}'' \times 11\frac{1}{4}'' \times 12\frac{1}{4}''$	2
		$\frac{3}{4}'' \times 2\frac{3}{4}'' \times 19\frac{3}{4}''$	2
		$\frac{3}{4}'' \times 6\frac{1}{2}'' \times 12\frac{1}{4}''$	6
		$\frac{3}{4}'' \times 9'' \times 12''$	2
		$\frac{3}{4}'' \times 11\frac{1}{4}'' \times 22''$	2
		$\frac{3}{4}'' \times 2\frac{3}{4}'' \times 20''$	2
		$\frac{3}{4}'' \times 6\frac{1}{2}'' \times 22''$	6
Drawer fronts:	Oak	$13/16'' \times 10\frac{13}{16}'' \times 15\frac{1}{2}''$	1
		$13/16'' \times 14'' \times 15\frac{1}{2}''$	1
		$13/16'' \times 3\frac{1}{2}'' \times 23''$	1
		$13/16'' \times 7\frac{3}{4}'' \times 15\frac{1}{2}''$	3
Desk feet:	Pine or fir	$2\frac{1}{4}'' \times 3\frac{1}{2}'' \times 19''$	2
Spacers:	Pine or fir	$1\frac{1}{2}'' \times 3\frac{1}{2}'' \times 18''$	8

Basic Cutting

Rip material for panel frames being sure to add $\frac{1}{8}''$ to specified width to allow for finishing edges on jointer.

Cut all frame parts to length. The two outside end panels (Illus. 4.2) are made $\frac{7}{8}''$ wider than the two inside panels (Illus. 4.3) to provide room for the back panel assembly (4.4) to be sandwiched between the two ends at back (Illus. 4.5, top view).

Panel Assembly

Plane off $\frac{1}{16}''$ from edges of each frame part with jointer.

Lay out the panel assemblies in proper order and mark for dowel holes. Glue and dowel panel frames (Illus. 4.6). Clamp with pipe clamps. Rough sand front and back surfaces after glue dries.

Rout around the inside front edge with a $\frac{3}{8}''$ rounding-over bit and cut a rabbet on the inside back edge of frame with router (Illus. 4.7).

Fine-sand all surfaces. Start with 100-grit paper, followed in order by 120 and 180.

Cut $\frac{1}{4}''$ plywood to fit in the rabbeted back side. Fine-sand the plywood, then secure the pieces in frame with wire brads.

Drawer Housing Cutting and Assembly

The structure of the drawer chests correspond at either end of desk. Facings, however, are made to accommodate different size drawers (Illus. 4.5, front view).

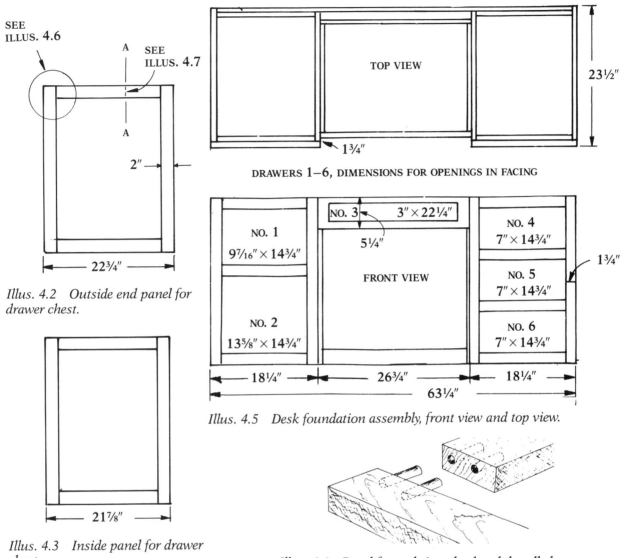

SEE ILLUS. 4.6

A   SEE ILLUS. 4.7

A

2"

22¾"

Illus. 4.2   Outside end panel for drawer chest.

TOP VIEW

23½"

1¾"

DRAWERS 1–6, DIMENSIONS FOR OPENINGS IN FACING

NO. 3   3" × 22¼"

NO. 1
9⁷⁄₁₆" × 14¾"

5¼"

NO. 4
7" × 14¾"

1¾"

FRONT VIEW

NO. 5
7" × 14¾"

NO. 2
13⅝" × 14¾"

NO. 6
7" × 14¾"

18¼"   26¾"   18¼"

63¼"

Illus. 4.5   Desk foundation assembly, front view and top view.

21⅞"

Illus. 4.3   Inside panel for drawer chest.

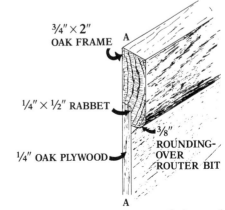

Illus. 4.6   Panel frame being glued and dowelled.

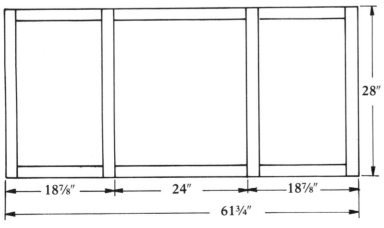

18⅞"   24"   18⅞"

61¾"

28"

Illus. 4.4   Back panel assembly.

¾" × 2"
OAK FRAME

A

¼" × ½" RABBET

⅜"
ROUNDING-
OVER
ROUTER BIT

¼" OAK PLYWOOD

A

Illus. 4.7   Cross section of plywood panel and frame construction.

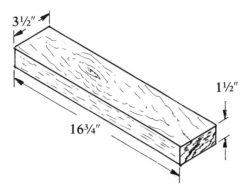

Illus. 4.8   Spacer board dimensions, for joining inside and end panels.

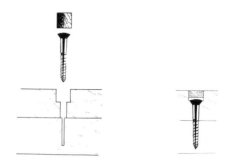

Illus. 4.9   Counterboring and covering screws with wood plugs.

Cut spacer boards to length (Illus. 4.8). These are used to secure the outside end panels to the inside panels to form box-like casings which will house drawers.

Counterbore and drill pilot holes for screws in the panels (Illus. 4.9). Assemble panels to make the two drawer chests, one for each end of desk. Glue plugs in counterbored holes to cover screwheads and sand them flush with frame surface.

Cut parts for middle drawer carriage. This will be secured between the two end drawer chests and will accommodate the small drawer above the desk leg space. Assemble parts with glue and screws. Sand top and bottom edges flush, then fine-sand front facing.

Rip materials for the drawer chest facings to width, allowing ⅛" for finishing on a jointer. Remove ¹⁄₁₆" from each edge of the boards on the jointer.

Lay out parts in proper order, and mark the locations of dowel holes. Assemble the drawer chest facings with glue and dowels, and then secure the assemblies with pipe clamps. Check that assembled facings are square before the glue sets. Rough-sand the back surface of each facing after the glue dries.

Counterbore and drill for screws, and then attach the facings to drawer chest. Glue wood plugs in the counterbored holes to cover screws. Sand plugs flush with the surface of the facings.

Desk Foundation Assembly

Secure the middle drawer case between the two end drawer chests with screws (Illus. 4.1). Attach back panel in place and secure with screws.

Drawer Cutting and Assembly

Cut drawer parts according to Table I, Part Sizes for Drawers.

TABLE I: PART SIZES FOR DRAWERS

Drawer	Ends (Make Two)	Side Rails (Make Two)	Front (Make One)	Bottom (Make One)
1	9" × 12¼"	9" × 22"	10³⁄₁₆" × 15½"	12⅞" × 21⅞"
2	11¼" × 12¼"	11¼" × 22"	14¹⁄₁₆" × 15½"	12⅞" × 21⅞"
3	2¾" × 19¾"	2¾" × 20"	23" × 3½"	20⅜" × 19⅛"
4	6½" × 12¼"	6½" × 22"	7¾" × 15½"	12⅞" × 21⅛"
5	6½" × 12¼"	6½" × 22"	7¾" × 15½"	12⅞" × 21⅛"
6	6½" × 12¼"	6½" × 22"	7¾" × 15½"	12⅞" × 21⅛"

Note: Sides and ends made from ¾" stock; front made from ¹³⁄₁₆" oak; bottom made from ¼" plywood.

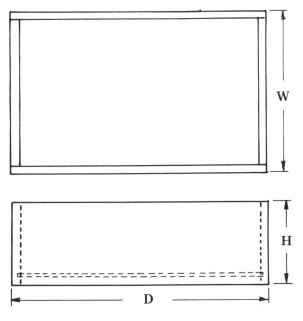

TABLE II: FINISHED DRAWER SIZES WITHOUT FRONT
(see drawing, Illus. 4.10)

Drawer	W Width	D Front to Back	H Height of Rail
1	13¾″	22″	9″
2	13¾″	22″	11¾″
3	21¾″	20″	2¾″
4	13¾″	22″	6½″
5	13¾″	22″	6½″
6	13¾″	22″	6½″

Illus. 4.10   Drawer sizes without front. See Table II.

Assemble the drawers referring to Table II, Finished Drawer Sizes Without Front (Illus. 4.10). Check square after assembly.

Attach the drawer fronts with screws driven from inside front of drawer (4.11). Rout around the front edges of each drawer (4.12). Fine-sand the drawer fronts.

Illus. 4.12   Routing edges of drawer front.

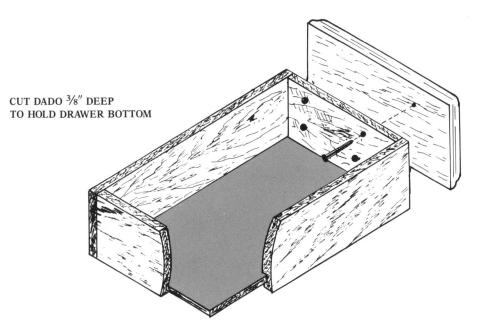

CUT DADO ⅜″ DEEP
TO HOLD DRAWER BOTTOM

Illus. 4.11   Attaching front to drawer assembly, with cutaway view of dadoed bottom construction.

Illus. 4.13   Side-mount drawer guides.

Secure side-mount drawer guides to drawer and chest according to accompanying directions (4.13).

Desk Top Assembly

Rip boards for the desk top (4.14). Smooth both edges of each board on jointer. Allow about one inch on width and length for cutting to exact size later.

Dry-clamp boards without dowels or glue to check for fit (Illus. 4.15). Mark the location of dowel holes while the boards are in the clamps. Drill dowel holes, then assemble boards with glue and dowels. Clamp again with pipe or bar clamps. Clamp each end of the boards with "C" clamps to prevent warping.

Rough-sand both bottom and top surfaces after glue dries. Cut top to size, leaving ⅛" all around for finishing.

Turn the top upside down, and secure a ½" × 1" strip all around the outside edges to provide extra thickness to the overhang (Illus. 4.14).

Finishing

Place the top on the desk and finish edges with a hand plane and sander. Rout around top edges with a ½" rounding-over bit. Fine-sand all exposed surfaces.

Now you are ready to make the feet (Illus. 4.16). Cut boards to rough size and glue together. Cut the feet to the finished size after the glue dries. Rout and sand edges to shape.

Attach the feet to the bottom of the drawer chests positioned so each is balanced both lengthwise and widthwise beneath its drawer chest. Apply stain and finish as you desire following the manufacturer's directions.

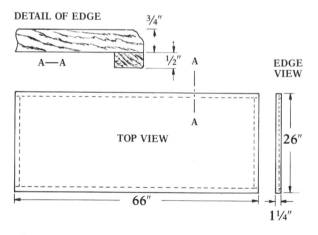

Illus. 4.14   Desk top dimensions and detail of thin wood strip beneath the outside edge.

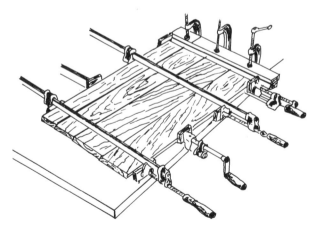

Illus. 4.15   Clamping boards for the desk top.

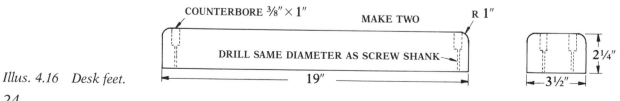

Illus. 4.16   Desk feet.

5 ◆ DESK TRAYS

Here is the perfect accessory for the handsome desk of the previous project; a pair of desk trays. But you needn't stop at two as any reasonable number can be made, for another desk at home or for the office. The trays are large enough to accommodate legal-sized as well as letter-sized documents. The trays pictured are made of walnut, but other woods will give equally fine results.

SUPPLIES

- Radial-arm saw or table saw
- Band saw or scroll saw
- Drill with $\frac{1}{16}''$ bit
- Finishing sander or sanding block
- Garnet paper in 80, 120, and 180 grits
- Nail set, No. 1
- Hammer
- 1″ wire brads
- Carpenter's glue
- Semi-gloss polyurethane finish
- 000 steel wool
- Jointer (optional)

Materials		Quantity
Sides	$\frac{1}{2}'' \times 3\frac{1}{2}'' \times 15''$	4
Ends	$\frac{1}{2}'' \times 3\frac{1}{2}'' \times 10''$	4
Bottoms	$\frac{1}{2}'' \times 10'' \times 14''$	2

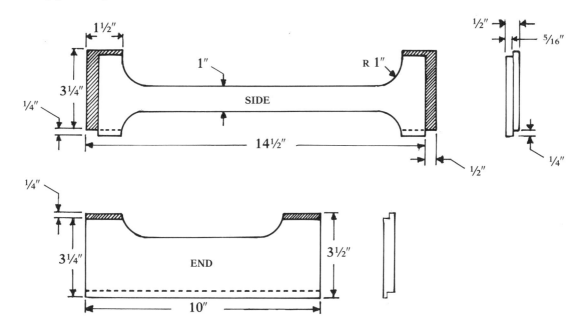

Illus. 5.1   Desk tray plans, dimensions of sides and ends.

Illus. 5.2 Sanding with a finishing sander.

INSTRUCTIONS

The construction of these exceptional desk trays is fairly straightforward, yet they require the care and attention that you would give a much larger project. After acquiring your starting materials and supplies, start by planing all of the boards to a ½" thickness.

Basic Cutting

Rip the boards to the specified widths. Cut the ends and sides to length (Illus. 5.1).

Cut rabbets along the edges of the boards as specified. The rabbets can be cut with either a table saw or jointer. On each end of the side boards use a radial-arm saw or table saw to cut the ½" rabbets.

Lay out the cutouts to be made on the sides and ends. Make the cuts with a band saw or scroll saw. Sand all saw marks from the edges, then sand all other surfaces (Illus. 5.2). Sand first with medium-grit garnet paper (80–100), followed with fine grit (120–180).

Assembly

Drill pilot holes in the rabbeted ends of the sides to accommodate one-inch wire brads (Illus. 5.3). Attach sides to ends with glue and wire brads (Illus. 5.4). Using a nail set, drive the heads of wire brads below the surface.

Illus. 5.3 Drilling pilot holes for wire brads.

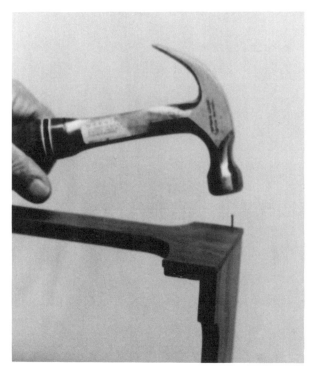

Illus. 5.4 Fastening side to end with glue and wire brads.

Cut the bottom board to fit inside. Drill pilot holes for securing the bottom board with wire brads (Illus. 5.5). Align the bottom board in place and secure. Sand all joints flush.

Finishing

Apply one coat of semi-gloss polyurethane finish. After the finish dries, cover the wire brad heads with colored putty, then apply additional coats of finish. Allow each coat to dry thoroughly before application of the next. Smooth the finish between coats with 000 steel wool.

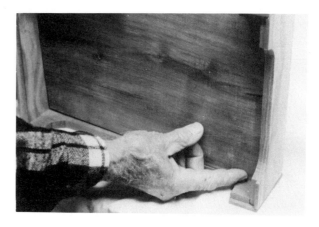

Illus. 5.5 Aligning bottom board ready to be nailed in place.

6 ◆ BOOKENDS

This attractive project allows you to use the design pictured as a point of departure for your own imagination. One of the big advantages of this approach to making these bookends is that you can select from odds and ends of wood that otherwise might be discarded. The final design will be most pleasing if woods with contrasting grain, color, and texture are used.

INSTRUCTIONS

Several gluing operations are necessary to make these bookends. To create the diagonal designs in the middle of each bookend, a variety of wood kinds and thicknesses are glued up depending on what is available. The glued-up stock is cut in sections at an angle, and thin pieces of wood—veneers—are used to set off the diagonal designs. No stain is needed; the contrasts come from the different woods used.

Basic Cutting

Plane materials to desired thickness for gluing up stock that will be cut for the diagonal designs. Cut boards to approximately the same dimensions, allowing enough extra length and width for truing up and finishing. Before applying glue, arrange the pieces in the order in which you wish to glue them.

Gluing and Sanding

Apply glue to one board at a time, stacking them in order as you proceed. Once the glue is applied to all joints, clamp the assembly with furniture clamps. Tap the boards with a mallet to keep them in line as the clamps are gradually tightened. Work alternately from clamp to clamp to help prevent the boards from sliding out of line.

After the glue dries, sand the sides down so that all edges are flush and the sides are flat.

Materials		Quantity
Walnut	⅜″ × 2¼″ × 6½″	6
Maple	¾″ × 2¼″ × 6½″	6
Red cedar	1″ × 2¼″ × 6½″	5
Basswood	¹⁄₁₆″ × 2¼″ × 6½″	4
Maple	⅜″ × 2¼″ × 6½″	2
Thin pieces of veneer, as desired		
Sheet metal for bases	4½″ wide	2

SUPPLIES

- Carpenter's glue
- 000 steel wool
- Garnet paper, medium (80–100) and fine (120–180)
- Semi-gloss polyurethane finish
- Furniture clamps
- Plane
- Table saw or radial-arm saw
- Mallet

28

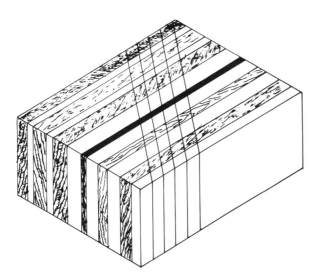

Illus. 6.1   Cutting diagonally across glued-up stock.

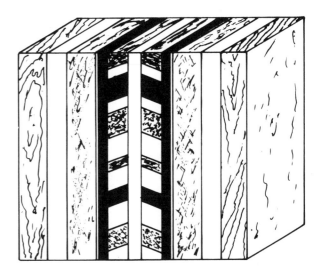

Illus. 6.2   Boards glued up to form a pattern of contrasting colors and textures.

Bookends Assembly

Cut sections of equal width from the glued-up boards (Illus. 6.1). To make the cuts, set the mitre of the saw on 110 degrees. You can vary this angle according to your own likes, but keep in mind that the greater the angle, the longer the sawed section will be.

Arrange these sections with other boards of equal dimensions and with surrounding pieces of veneer to form a pleasing design. After you are satisfied with the design, glue and clamp the elements together (Illus. 6.2) in a similar manner to the earlier gluing operation.

Sand the sides down flat, and then square the ends. Sand all surfaces with medium grit garnet paper (80–100), followed with fine grit paper (120–180).

Using a jointer or table saw, cut a section from about two-thirds of the bottom to accommodate the sheet metal base (Illus. 6.3).

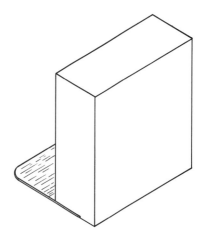

Illus. 6.3   End view of bookend, showing cutaway section on bottom to accommodate sheet metal base.

Finishing

Spray three coats of semi-gloss polyurethane finish, allowing each coat to dry overnight before applying the next. Smooth the surface between coats with 000 steel wool.

7 ✦ ENTERTAINMENT CENTER

To help your home have a warm country feel, you might consider constructing this beautiful cabinet that opens easily for television viewing. This sturdy piece of oak furniture has room for not only a large-size TV, but also your VCR or cable box, if you have them. There is still ample space left for storing odd items like the candleware pictured. Two huge drawers can house such items as blank cassettes and your videotape collection. You may even be inspired to construct a tray similar to the one pictured that fits exactly in the drawer and lifts out easily with your videotapes.

INSTRUCTIONS

The cabinet is no more complicated than a basic box-like construction (Illus. 7.1). The other elements are in themselves straightforward to make. The mouldings are all the same and are simply attached to the facing of the cabinet. The scalloped doors are frame-and-panel construction, and the drawers are boxes with added drawer fronts.

Materials			Quantity
Sides:	Oak plywood	$3/4'' \times 23'' \times 66\frac{1}{2}''$	2
Ends and middle shelf:	Oak plywood	$3/4'' \times 22\frac{3}{4}'' \times 27\frac{1}{2}''$	3
Shelves (adjustable):	Oak plywood	$3/4'' \times 22'' \times 27\frac{3}{8}''$	2
Back:	Oak plywood	$1/4'' \times 28\frac{1}{4}'' \times 65\frac{3}{4}''$	1
Doors:	Oak	$3/4'' \times 3'' \times 34''$	4
	Oak	$3/4'' \times 5'' \times 8''$	4
	Oak plywood	$1/4'' \times 11'' \times 30''$	2
Drawers:	White pine	$3/4'' \times 7'' \times 24''$	8
	Plywood	$3/4'' \times 24'' \times 24''$	2
	Oak	$3/4'' \times 8'' \times 27''$	2
Facings:	Oak	$3/4'' \times 2'' \times 66\frac{1}{2}''$	2
	Oak	$3/4'' \times 2'' \times 25''$	3
	Oak	$3/4'' \times 3\frac{1}{2}'' \times 25''$	1
	Oak	$3/4'' \times 4'' \times 25''$	1

SUPPLIES

- Two door handles
- Two pairs side-mount drawer glides
- Four drawer handles
- Sixteen (⅜″ × 2″) dowel pins
- Carpenter's glue
- Hinges
- Table saw
- Scroll saw
- Drill
- Dado blades for table saw
- Router
- Rabbeting bit
- ⅜″ Roman ogee bit
- ¾″ rounding-over bit
- 1¼″ sheetrock screws
- ¾″ wire brads
- No. 6 finish nails or screws
- Shelf rails
- Sandpaper
- Furniture clamps
- Stain
- Semi-gloss polyurethane finish

Basic cutting

Cut the ¾″ plywood to size for the sides, top, and bottom (Illus. 7.1). Counterbore ⅜″ × ⅜″ holes for screws. Drill a ³⁄₁₆″ pilot hole through the remaining thickness. Using dado blades on the table saw, cut ¼″ × ⅝″ rabbets on the inside of the ¾″ plywood to accommodate adjustable shelf rails in the top section of the cabinet.

Cabinet Assembly

Fasten the sides to the top and bottom with 1¼″ sheetrock screws and glue. Using a rabbeting bit, rout a ¼″ × ¼″ rabbet around inside edges on the back side to accommodate the ¼″ plywood back.

Measure for the location of the middle shelf. Note that the shelves must be cut ¼″ less in depth to allow for installation of the plywood back. Secure middle shelf with screws.

Glue a wood plug in each counterbored hole to cover screwheads (Illus. 7.2). After glue dries, sand the wood plug flush with side surfaces.

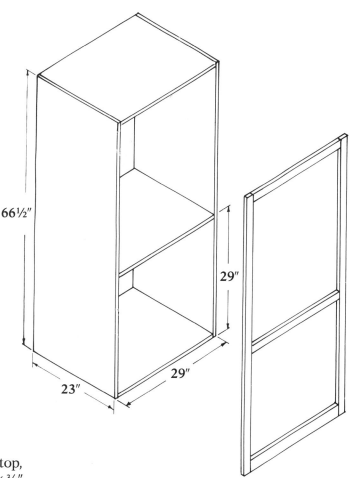

Illus. 7.1   Basic cabinet box with dimensions and showing partially assembled facings.

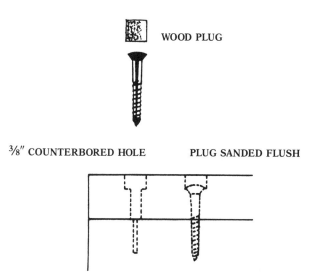

WOOD PLUG

⅜″ COUNTERBORED HOLE   PLUG SANDED FLUSH

Illus. 7.2   Covering screwheads with wood plugs.

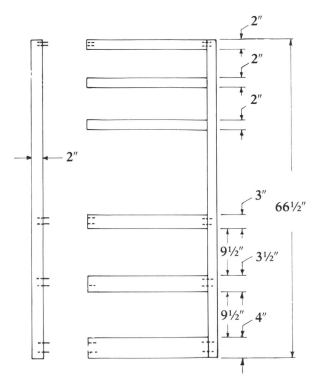

Illus. 7.3   Facings with dimensions and dowel locations. The top two shelves are adjustable, not attached to facings.

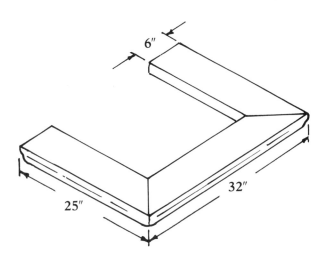

Illus. 7.4   Mouldings for top and bottom of cabinet. Before cutting to size, rout along one edge with a ⅜" Roman ogee bit.

Facings

Cut facing parts to size and lay out and drill dowel holes (Illus. 7.3). Assemble facings with glue, dowels, and furniture clamps. Sand back side of facings flat. Counterbore and drill pilot holes for mounting facings to cabinet front with glue and screws. Secure one side of facings, then check squareness of cabinet before securing the remaining side and ends.

Mouldings

Rip top and bottom boards for making mouldings (Illus. 7.4). Rout along one edge with a ⅜" Roman ogee bit. Cut parts to size, allowing a 1½" overhang at both the top and bottom of the cabinet. Mitre the corners, and then attach to the cabinet with screws and glue. Using a ¾" rounding-over bit, cut moulding to go under the overhang (Illus. 7.5).

Door Assembly

Enlarge the door pattern (Illus. 7.6) to full size. Cut boards for making the frame. Leave enough width to fit the scalloped door pattern. Glue, dowel, and clamp the door frames. After the glue dries, saw the inside scallops of the frame on a scroll saw.

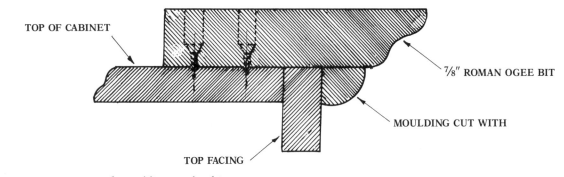

TOP OF CABINET

⅞" ROMAN OGEE BIT

MOULDING CUT WITH

TOP FACING

Illus. 7.5   Cross section of moulding and cabinet parts.

32

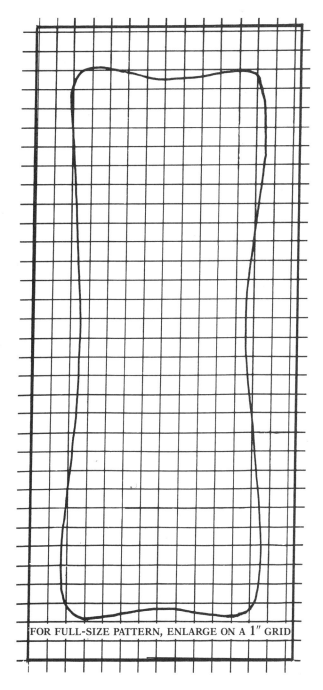

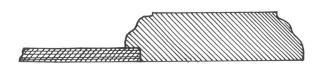

Illus. 7.7   Cross section of door panel frame. Front edges are routed with a ⅜″ Roman ogee bit.

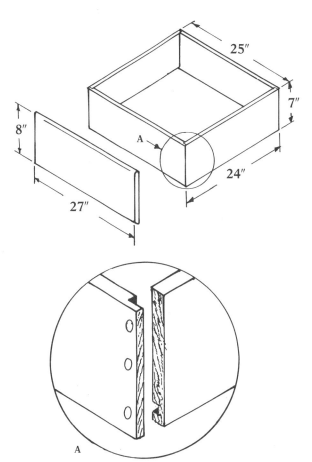

Illus. 7.8   Drawer construction with dimensions.

Illus. 7.6   Pattern for doors.

Sand all surfaces, then rout a rabbet on the back side to accommodate a ¼″ plywood panel. Rout the front edges of frame with a ⅜″ Roman ogee bit (Illus. 7.7). Install the ¼″ plywood panels with ¾″ wire brads.

Mount the doors to cabinet facings with pin hinges.

Drawer Assembly

Cut drawer parts to size (Illus. 7.8). Note that the drawer width must be one inch less than the drawer opening in the cabinet to allow for mounting of side-mount drawer glides.

Cut a ¼″ rabbet at the bottom of all four parts. Cut the ¼″ plywood bottom. Cut rabbets for lap joints on each end of drawer sides. Assemble the drawer box with glue and No. 6 finish nails or screws.

Cut the drawer fronts to size, and sand. Rout around the front edges with the ⅜″ Roman ogee bit. Mount the fronts to the drawer boxes,

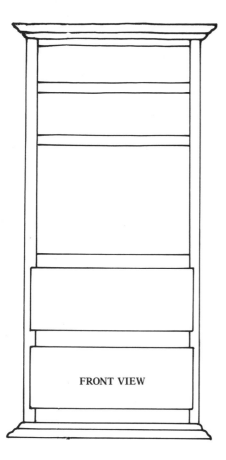
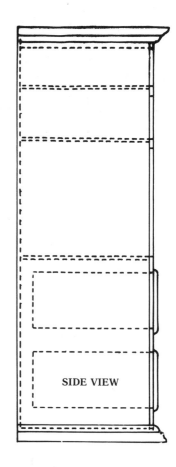

FRONT VIEW

SIDE VIEW

Illus. 7.9   Finished cabinet.

driving screws from the inside. To allow for later adjustments of drawer front, do not glue.

Install the drawers with side-mount drawer glides according to the manufacturer's instructions.

Adjustable Shelves

Install shelf rails for adjustable shelves. Cut shelf boards to size, and secure the facing boards to the front edge with screws covered with wood plugs.

Finishing

Check all surfaces of cabinet and sand where necessary before applying finish (Illus. 7.9). Apply stain according to the manufacturer's instructions. After the stain dries, apply a semi-gloss polyurethane finish.

8 ◆ SWINGING CRADLE

The swinging motion of this cradle will help baby go to sleep in style, and its lovely, smooth wood makes it a potential family heirloom. Wild cherry wood was used here, but any hardwood that you find pleasing will do as well.

SUPPLIES

- Crib bumpers
- Four ¾″ No. 6 round-head screws
- Four 2″ No. 10 flat-head screws
- 1 box 1½″ No. 8 hardboard screws
- Wire brads
- Garnet paper, various grits
- Carpenter's glue
- Table saw
- Wood lathe
- Drill and various bits
- Router and various bits
- Sander and sanding belts
- Finish (as desired)

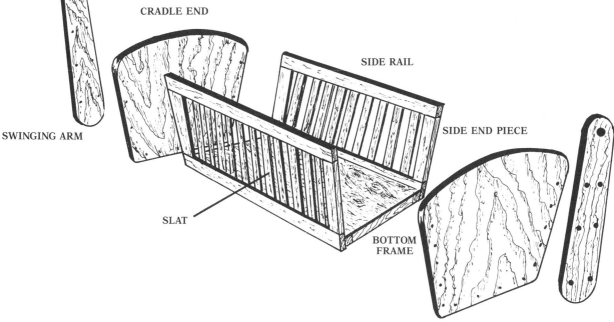

Illus. 8.1   Exploded view of main elements of cradle, excluding stand assembly.

Materials		Minimum size	Quantity
End assembly:	Cradle end	$^{13}/_{16}'' \times 18'' \times 22''$	2
	Swinging arm	$^{13}/_{16}'' \times 5'' \times 22''$	2
Side assembly:	Slat	$^{1}/_{2}'' \times 9^{1}/_{2}'' \times 1^{1}/_{4}''$	22
	Side rail	$1^{1}/_{8}'' \times 2^{1}/_{8}'' \times 30''$	4
	Side end piece	$1^{1}/_{8}'' \times 2^{1}/_{8}'' \times 10''$	4
	Spacer block	$^{1}/_{2}'' \times ^{1}/_{2}'' \times 1''$	48
Bottom assembly:	Frame side piece	$1^{1}/_{8}'' \times 1^{1}/_{2}'' \times 30''$	2
	Frame cross-member	$1^{1}/_{8}'' \times 1^{1}/_{2}'' \times 12''$	4
	Plywood bottom	$^{1}/_{2}'' \times 14'' \times 30''$	1
Stand assembly:	Upright	$^{13}/_{16}'' \times 6'' \times 35''$	2
	Feet	$^{13}/_{16}'' \times 5'' \times 24''$	2
	Main cross-member	$1^{1}/_{8}'' \times 4^{1}/_{4}'' \times 36''$	1
	Outer cross-member	$1^{1}/_{8}'' \times 2^{1}/_{4}'' \times 36''$	2
Bearing assembly:	Shaft	$2'' \times 2'' \times 6''$	2
	Washer	$^{13}/_{16}'' \times 2'' \times 12''$	2
	Split collar	$^{13}/_{16}'' \times 2'' \times 12''$	2

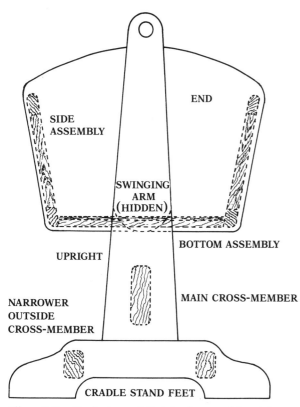

Illus. 8.2 End view of finished assembly with construction elements identified.

Once the project is completed, you should add crib bumpers, obtainable from department and specialty stores. The design allows the easy assembly and disassembly of separate units to form the completed cradle.

INSTRUCTIONS

There are five basic elements in the construction of this swinging cradle (Illus. 8.1). They are the end assemblies, the sides, the bottom, the stand assembly (Illus. 8.2) to support the cradle, and, lastly, the bearing assembly that allows the cradle to swing. Each of these elements is assembled separately and later combined to complete the cradle project.

For each element screws are used that should be countersunk and covered with plugs (Illus. 8.3), with the single exception of the small screws securing the bearing collar. All surfaces to be finished should be progressively sanded so that each element of construction is ready for finishing, except surfaces where screw plugs will need to be sanded flush. Proceed from paper with grits ranging from 50 to

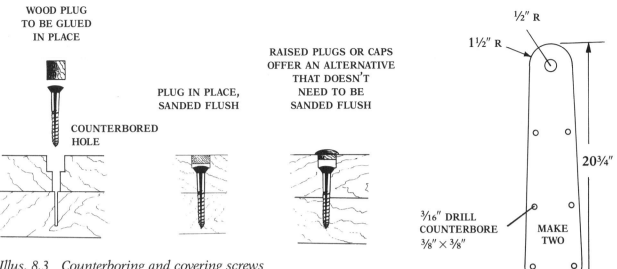

Illus. 8.3   Counterboring and covering screws with wood plugs.

WOOD PLUG
TO BE GLUED
IN PLACE

COUNTERBORED
HOLE

PLUG IN PLACE,
SANDED FLUSH

RAISED PLUGS OR CAPS
OFFER AN ALTERNATIVE
THAT DOESN'T
NEED TO BE
SANDED FLUSH

½″ R

1½″ R

20¾″

³⁄₁₆″ DRILL
COUNTERBORE
³⁄₈″ × ³⁄₈″

MAKE
TWO

2⅜″ R

DO NOT ROUT EDGE
WHERE ARM AND
END BOARD JOIN.

Illus. 8.5   Cradle bed swinging arm.

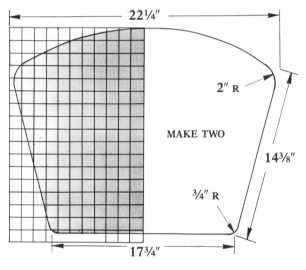

Illus. 8.4   Pattern for cradle ends.

22¼″

2″ R

MAKE TWO

14⅜″

¾″ R

17¾″

80 for a rough sanding through several sanding steps to a grit range of 100 to 180 or finer.

Cradle End and Swinging Arm Assemblies

Cut materials to the rough lengths required to make the cradle ends (Illus. 8.4). Dowel and glue the pieces edge-to-edge to satisfy the width needed. After the glue dries, rough-sand both surfaces.

Following the pattern, cut the ends to shape. Sand the edges, then rout around both edges to give a ¼″ radius. Fine-sand the edges and both surfaces.

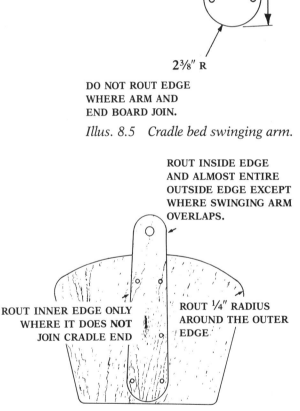

ROUT INSIDE EDGE
AND ALMOST ENTIRE
OUTSIDE EDGE EXCEPT
WHERE SWINGING ARM
OVERLAPS.

ROUT INNER EDGE ONLY
WHERE IT DOES NOT
JOIN CRADLE END

ROUT ¼″ RADIUS
AROUND THE OUTER
EDGE

Illus. 8.6   Cradle end and swinging arm assembly.

Cut the swinging arm to shape (Illus. 8.5). Counterbore for screws, then drill pilot holes. Bore a one inch hole that will later accommodate bearing shaft. Rout a ¼″ radius on edges, and fine-sand all surfaces. Attach each swinging arm to one of the cradle ends (Illus. 8.6).

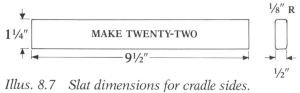

1¼" MAKE TWENTY-TWO

9½"

⅛" R

½"

Illus. 8.7   Slat dimensions for cradle sides.

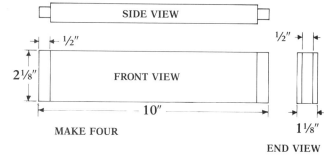

SIDE VIEW

½" ½"

2⅛" FRONT VIEW

10"

MAKE FOUR

END VIEW

1⅛"

Illus. 8.8   End piece dimensions for cradle sides.

Assembling the Sides

Cut the 22 slats to sizes, and rough-sand all surfaces (Illus. 8.7). Cut four pieces to shape for the cradle side end pieces (Illus. 8.8). Sand all surfaces, and cut a tongue on each end of these end pieces. Cut four pieces for the top and bottom side rails, and cut a groove ½" by ½" in each rail (Illus. 8.9). Rout the edges of all these parts with a rounding-over bit as appropriate. Fine-sand all parts.

Glue only one end piece to a pair of rails, securing with a furniture clamp. Slide the eleven slats into the grooves in the rails, letting them stack up against the secured end piece. Glue and clamp the other end piece in place.

Cut 48 spacer blocks to fill the groove between slats ½" by ½" and one inch long. Drill a hole through each spacer block to accommo-

date a small wire brad. Fine-sand these blocks. Starting at one end, secure spacer blocks at the top and bottom in the groove between the end piece and the first slat. Place a small amount of glue on the bottom of each spacer block before securing in the groove with a small wire brad. Set the nail through the hole in the spacer block using a nail set so that the head sets slightly below the surface.

Work towards the other end until the last slat is reached. The last pair of spacer blocks may need to be sanded to fit, or another pair of longer blocks may need to be made.

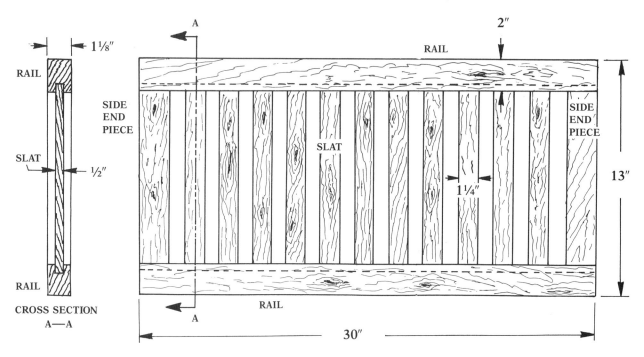

Illus. 8.9   Cradle side assembly dimensions with cross-section view (A—A).

38

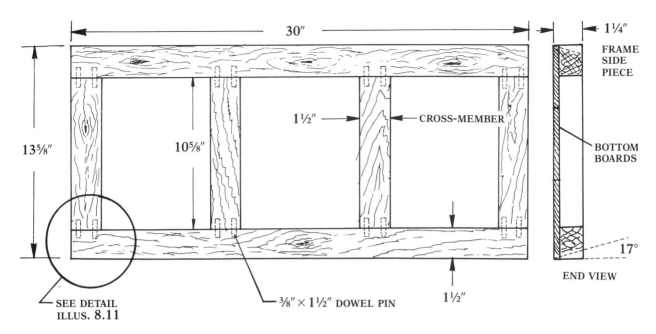

Illus. 8.10   Cradle bottom dimensions and assembly details.

Constructing the Cradle Bottom

Cut the bottom frame pieces to size (Illus. 8.10). Assemble the bottom frame before cutting the indicated edge angle of 17 degrees. This will assure an accurate fit and smooth surface for attaching the sides later.

Dowel and glue the cross-members to the frame side pieces (Illus. 8.11). Cut bottom boards to fit, and attach them over the framework with screws. Fill counterbored screw holes with plugs and sand flush after glue dries. Fine-sand the entire surface of the bottom. Rip the edges off to the 17 degree angle.

Making the Cradle Stand

Cut pieces for the three cross-members to a 36″ length (about an inch longer than specified) so that they can be fitted later. Cut one piece 4¼″ wide (Illus. 8.12) and two 2¼″ wide. Cut two pieces for the feet (Illus. 8.13). Lay out and cut two pieces for the upright members for the stand (Illus. 8.14).

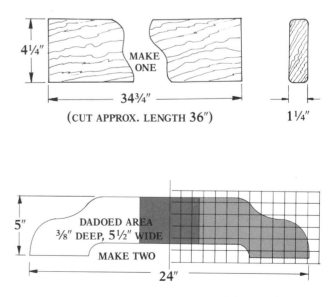

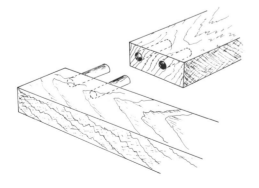

Illus. 8.11   Dowelling detail for cradle bottom.

Illus. 8.13   Pattern for cradle stand feet. Enlarge to a one-inch grid for full-size pattern.

39

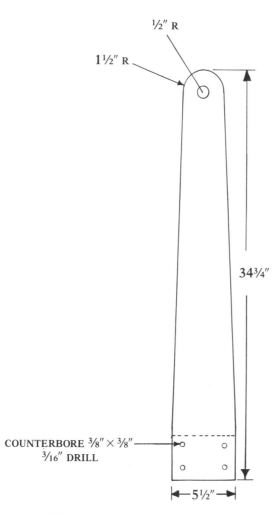

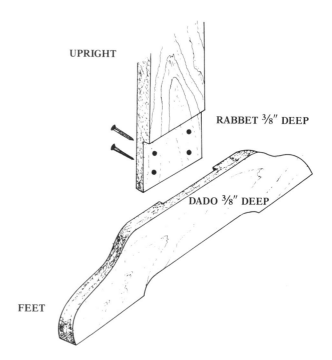

½" R

1½" R

34¾"

COUNTERBORE ⅜" × ⅜"
³⁄₁₆" DRILL

5½"

Illus. 8.14 Layout for upright member of cradle stand.

UPRIGHT

RABBET ⅜" DEEP

DADO ⅜" DEEP

FEET

Illus. 8.15 Upright and foot assembly detail.

Rough-sand all surfaces, and rout edges as indicated. Counterbore and drill for screws in the upright members, and bore a one-inch hole in each upright member to accommodate the bearing shaft.

Dado and rabbet the portions of the feet and upright members that will interlock (Illus. 8.15). Note that the interlocking portions are only ⅜" deep, which is less than halfway through each board. This will allow the rounded, routed edge to show. Attach the uprights to the feet with glue and screws, covering the holes with plugs.

The cross-members for the stand are not attached until the entire cradle bed is being assembled, to allow accurate fitting.

Bearing Shaft and Spacer Assembly

Use the same material as used for the other elements of the cradle to make the bearing assembly. The parts are turned on a wood lathe, with care given to the dimensions specified and the tolerances (+ or −) that are indicated (Illus. 8.16). Some parts can vary from the given size; some can only be smaller such as the bearing shaft, and some can only be larger such as the spacer ring.

Joining the Cradle Bed Elements

Align the sides against the bottom assembly (Illus. 8.1), and mark the bottom rails to allow screws to enter the bottom framework in the middle of the frame piece. Counterbore and drill pilot holes along the bottom rail of the sides. Drive the screws, making sure that each side and the bottom are flush at the ends. To assure proper alignment secure the sides and bottom with clamps while the screws are driven.

Attach the ends to the sides and bottom with screws, sanding wood plugs flush with end pieces.

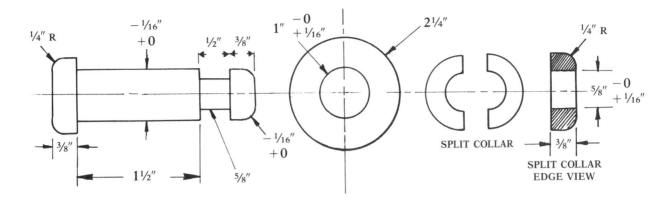

Illus. 8.16   Specifications for turning bearing shaft spacer assembly on wood lathe.

Completing the Stand

With the cradle bed complete, the stand can be accurately assembled by following a simple formula. Find the length of the main cross-member by first measuring the total distance from the outside of one swinging arm of the cradle bed assembly to the outside of the other swinging arm. Allow for the two spacer washers of each bearing assembly by adding twice the washer thickness to the above measurement, and then add an extra ⅛" to allow some room for fitting.

Note that the two narrower cross-members must be cut to a greater length than the wider main cross-member. These two outside cross-members can only be fitted properly after the middle one is installed.

Attach the middle cross-member between the uprights. Measure between both feet support pieces at the locations where the narrower cross-members are to join (Illus. 8.2). If the measurements on each side are different, simply split the difference and the stand will be true. Cut the narrower cross-members to length, and secure them at the proper locations between the feet support pieces.

Finishing

Apply finish before the final assembly stage. Be sure to follow the manufacturer's directions, but finish the piece according to your own desires. The completed cradle pictured was simply hand-rubbed with tung oil, which enhances the natural lustre of the wood.

Completing Cradle Bed Assembly

The last step is to hang the cradle in the stand, and for this you may find it is easiest to enlist the help of one or two "assistants." Hold the cradle bed in place between the stand and assemble the bearing shaft and washers (Illus. 8.17). Secure by pressing each retaining washer half into place around the undercut shaft end, and fasten with ¾" round-head screws.

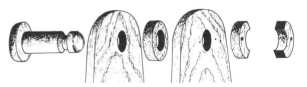

Illus. 8.17   Installing the bearing shaft, spacer, and retaining washer halves.

9 ◆ BLANKET CHEST

This handsome oak blanket chest deserves a prominent place in your home. Not only will this chest offer convenient storage for quilts and blankets, but it also protects and preserves them because it has an inner lining of cedar. You can locate this chest almost anywhere since its simple but elegant design will fit in with any decor.

MATERIALS

- Oak lumber
- Dowels
- ¼" Oak plywood
- Wood plugs
- Red cedar boards

SUPPLIES

- Table saw
- Router, ¼" rounding-over bit
- Glue
- Clamps
- Screws
- Sandpaper
- Piano hinge
- Wire brads
- Stain
- Varnish

INSTRUCTIONS

The construction of the chest is a simple panelled box with lid (Illus. 9.1). The panel frames are oak lumber cut to size, and the panels are ¼" oak plywood set into rabbets. The lining is made from tightly set red cedar boards that are glued and nailed in place. Plan to finish the oak part of the chest after assembly but before the red cedar lining has been installed. Be careful that you do not apply any finish to the red cedar itself or its protective properties will be spoiled.

Basic Cutting

Rip materials for framing sides and ends. Cut framing materials to length and smooth edges (Illus. 9.2).

Lay frame parts, one at a time, on a smooth flat surface and arrange in position. Mark each board to identify it as a part of that

Illus. 9.1   Exploded view of basic chest construction.

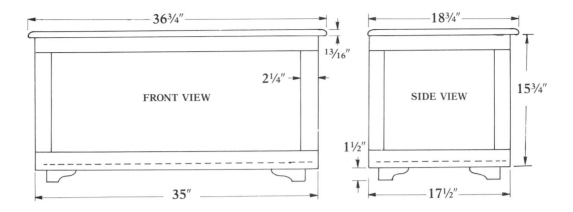

FRONT VIEW

SIDE VIEW

Illus. 9.2   Blanket chest dimensions.

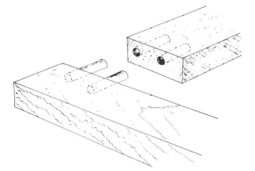

Illus. 9.3   Dowel holes and dowels join the frame.

particular frame. For example, all boards in the first frame might be marked with the letter A; all boards of the second frame might be marked with the letter B, etc.

Frame Assembly

Arrange each joint of frame, one at a time, in its exact finished position and mark location of dowel holes (Illus. 9.3). Drill holes for the dowels. Assemble the frames with glue and dowel pins, then clamp with furniture clamps.

After glue dries, sand front and back surfaces of the frame. Rout a radius around the inside front corner of each frame with a ¼″ rounding-over bit. Rout a rabbet on the inside back corner of each frame to accommodate the ¼″ oak plywood which is used for panelling the sides and ends.

Cut oak plywood to fit each frame, then sand the outside surface with fine grit paper before securing it in the back side of the frame using wire brads.

Assembling the Chest Box

Cut a rabbet along each end of the sides (Illus. 9.4). Assemble sides to ends with glue and screws. Glue wood plugs in each counterbored hole to cover the screws. Leave each plug protruding from the hole to allow sanding flush after glue dries.

Cut the bottom board to fit inside the sides and ends. Fasten the bottom securely in place with screws as described above. Sand all joints and plugs flush with the surrounding wood.

Gluing-up the Chest Top

Dowel and glue boards together edgewise for making the top. Clamp with furniture clamps. Sand both the top and bottom surfaces of the glued-up boards to be used for top, then cut to size according to drawings (Illus. 9.2).

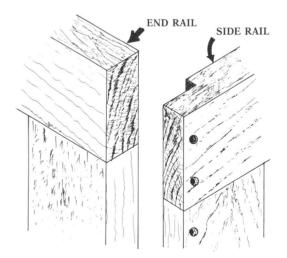

END RAIL   SIDE RAIL

Illus. 9.4   Joining side to end.

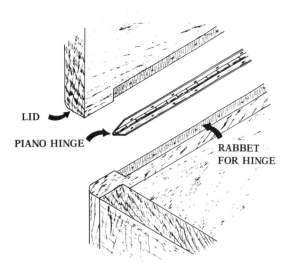

LID

PIANO HINGE

RABBET
FOR HINGE

Cut a rabbet in the lid and back rail to accommodate a piano hinge (Illus. 9.5). Rout around top edge of the lid with a ⅜″ rounding-over bit, then attach the lid to the back rail of the chest.

Finishing

Cut parts for legs (Illus. 9.6) and handles (Illus. 9.7). Attach these parts to the chest with screws, and then fine-sand all surfaces of the chest.

Apply stain and allow it to dry thoroughly before applying finish. Apply finish of your choice following the manufacturer's suggested methods.

Illus. 9.5   Placing hinge on back rail and lid.

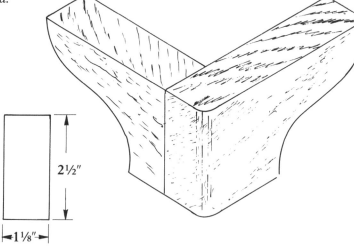

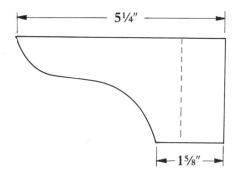

5¼″

2½″

1⅝″

1⅛″

Illus. 9.6   Leg plans and assembly.

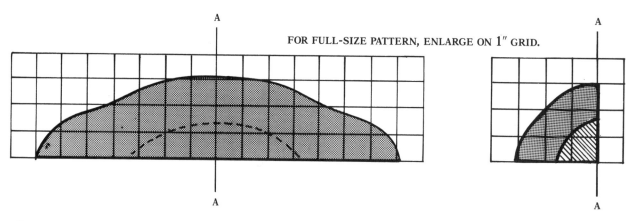

A

A

FOR FULL-SIZE PATTERN, ENLARGE ON 1″ GRID.

A

A

Illus. 9.7   Handle design and cross section.

44

Installing Cedar Lining

Cut red cedar boards to line bottom of the chest. Secure with glue and small wire brads (Illus. 9.8). Line inside ends, then inside sides. Note: Do not apply finish to the lining. To help support the lid when you open it, be sure to mount a sliding bracket heavy enough to offer proper support (Illus. 9.9).

Illus. 9.9   Detail of hinge and lid bracket support.

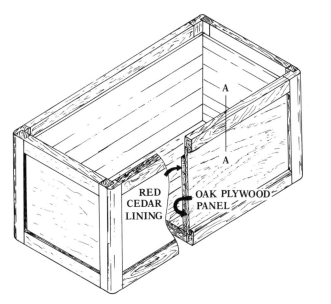

Illus. 9.8   Cutaway view of chest with inner red cedar lining.

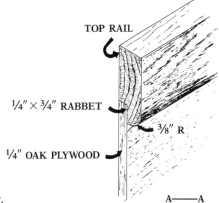

10 ◆ DOLL CRADLE

This doll cradle is straightforward to put together and will provide hours of fun to the recipient. The cradle pictured is made of pine and fits small dolls. You can use any wood and stain or paint (always use nontoxic materials) as you desire. A special touch might be to paint the child's name on the canopy or the foot of the cradle.

MATERIALS

- Wood lumber (variety, as desired)
- Individual specifications on part drawings

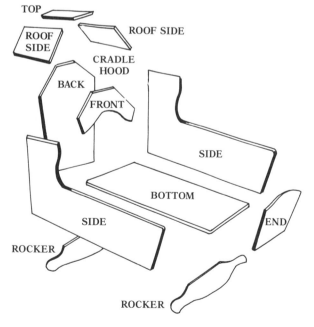

Illus. 10.1 Exploded view of doll cradle construction.

SUPPLIES

- Garnet paper, 80-120 and 180-220 grit
- Graphite paper
- 1¼" and 1" No. 6 flat-head screws
- Wood file
- Plane
- Table saw
- Router
- ¼" and ½" rounding-over bits
- Stain
- Poltyurethane varnish

INSTRUCTIONS

The cradle is composed of eleven pieces (Illus. 10.1), all of which are made from solid lumber. Of these pieces, some are essentially duplicates, so the construction actually involves only eight different parts. Assembly proceeds in three stages. The sides are assembled, then the bottom and rockers are put in place. Finally, the hood and roof pieces are placed and fitted.

Basic Cutting

Enlarge all of the patterns to full size (Illus. 10.2–10.9). Prepare the lumber to the proper thickness, if necessary. Cut all of the parts to shape, then sand the surfaces, including the edges, with medium-grit garnet paper (80-120).

Rout around the edges as specified using a ½" rounding-over bit. Fine-sand all parts with garnet paper (180-220).

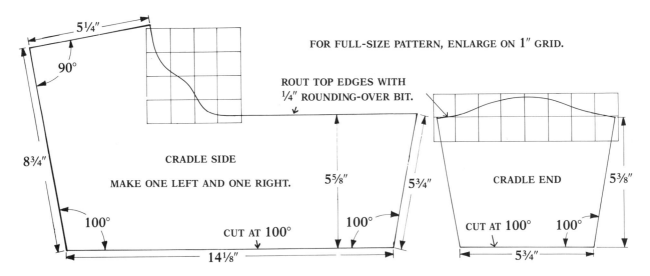

Illus. 10.2   Pattern and dimensions for cradle sides.

Illus. 10.4   Pattern and dimensions for cradle end.

Cradle Body Assembly

Use glue sparingly and carefully if you plan to stain the wood. Use screws, covered with wood plugs, to assemble the sides (Illus. 10.2) to the back (Illus. 10.3). Attach the cradle (Illus. 10.4). Sand the sides flush with the back and end, then rout each corner using a ¼" rounding-over bit.

Cradle Bottom and Rocker Assembly

Attach the bottom (Illus. 10.5) to the cradle body, using screws and being careful to allow for the slant of the sides. Use the longer 1¼" No. 6 flat-head screws. Attach the rockers (Illus. 10.6) to the bottom using the same screws.

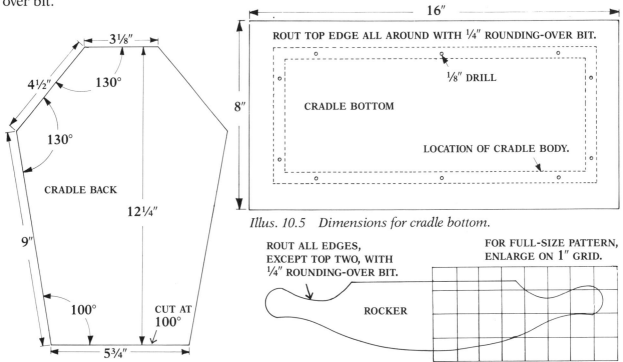

Illus. 10.5   Dimensions for cradle bottom.

Illus. 10.3   Dimensions for cradle back.

Illus. 10.6   Pattern and dimensions for rockers.

47

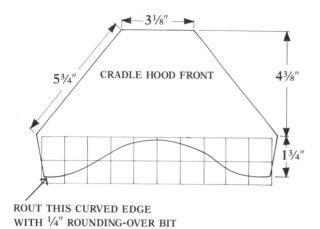

ROUT THIS CURVED EDGE
WITH ¼" ROUNDING-OVER BIT

FOR FULL-SIZE PATTERN, ENLARGE ON 1" GRID.

Illus. 10.7   Pattern and dimensions for cradle hood front.

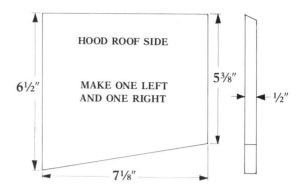

Illus. 10.8   Dimensions for sides of hood roof.

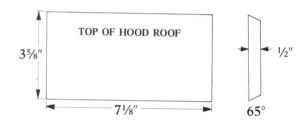

Illus. 10.9   Dimensions for top of hood roof.

Cradle Hood Assembly

Position the front of the hood (Illus. 10.7) between the sides and check for a proper fit. Make any necessary adjustments using a wood file and garnet paper. Attach the fitted front hood piece to both sides using 1" No. 6 screws.

Fit the sides of the hood roof (Illus. 10.8), and before final attachment shape the top of the hood roof as required. Once the roof pieces have been fitted, attach them to the cradle assembly using 1" No. 6 screws.

Finishing

Fine-sand all of the surfaces once more, making sure everything is smooth and flush. Once you are happy with all the surfaces and joints, apply stain to color, if desired. Then apply polyurethane varnish, taking care to sand two or three times between coats with fine-sand paper or, preferably, steel wool.

11 ◆ COAT RACK

Outfit your entranceway or back door passage with a handsome, sensible oak coat rack. In addition to pegs for outerwear or sweaters, there are handy shelves for stashing things and a swing-down drawer that makes a perfect bin for gloves, hats, and other necessities. This storage solution will lend your vestibule a traditional air while helping you and your family organize and keep track of belongings.

SUPPLIES

- 1¼″ No. 9 screws (46)
- Two ½″ × 2″ dowel pins
- Two ½″ oak buttons
- Carpenter's glue
- Saw
- Drill
- Router
- ⅜″ Roman ogee router bit
- ¼″ rounding-over bit
- Lathe (optional)
- Handle and coat hanger pegs, manufactured (optional)
- Garnet paper in coarse, medium, and fine grits
- 0000 steel wool
- Graphite transfer paper

INSTRUCTIONS

This coat rack consists of two assemblies. The main assembly is the oak shelf unit, into which the swing-down drawer unit is mounted. The drawer unit is a slanted box made of pine with an oak drawer front. The drawer is secured in the shelf unit with ½″ dowel pins that can be removed.

FOR FULL-SIZE PATTERN, ENLARGE ON 1″ GRID.

SIDE   SHELVES

MIDDLE BACK PIECE

BOTTOM BOARD   TOP BOARD

3½″   3⅜″   10⅝″   4″   5⅝″

½″   ¾″   ¾″   1⅜″

Illus. 11.1 Pattern for sides showing location of shelf and back parts. Actual coat hanger pegs used determine hole indicated by dotted lines on bottom board.

49

Materials			Quantity
Shelf assembly (oak):			
	Sides	³⁄₄″ × 9³⁄₈″ × 31½″	2
	Shelves	³⁄₄″ × 8″ × 26⁷⁄₈″	2
	Top	³⁄₄″ × 6½″ × 26⁷⁄₈″	1
	Bottom	³⁄₄″ × 6½″ × 26⁷⁄₈″	1
	Middle	³⁄₄″ × 4¾″ × 26⁷⁄₈″	1
Drawer box (pine):			
	Ends	³⁄₄″ × 8½″ × 6¼″	2
	Back	³⁄₄″ × 6½″ × 26¼″	1
	Box front	³⁄₄″ × 8½″ × 26¼″	1
Drawer front (oak):		³⁄₄″ × 9″ × 26¾″	1
Turning (pine):	(Optional)		
	Coat hanger pegs	1¼″ × 1¼″ × 5½″	5
	Handle	1¼″ × 1¼″ × 13″	1

Basic Cutting

Enlarge the patterns for the two sides (Illus. 11.1), and for the top board (Illus. 11.2) and bottom board (Illus. 11.3). Transfer the patterns to wood and cut these parts. Bore holes in the bottom board for coat hanger pegs according to what you have available or can turn.

Cut the two shelves and the middle back piece following the dimensions in the materials list. Sand all surfaces, first with coarse grit garnet paper followed with medium and fine grits.

Preparation and Shelf Assembly

Rout the front edges of the shelves and the decorative cuts on the top and bottom boards with a ³⁄₈″ Roman ogee bit. Rout the front edges of the sides with a ¼″ rounding-over bit.

Counterbore holes ³⁄₈″ by ³⁄₈″ at all screw locations in the side parts, drilling a ³⁄₁₆″ pilot hole through into the joining piece. Attach the back parts and the shelves between the sides, starting with the top board and working down (Illus. 11.4). Glue wood plugs to cover the screws, leaving the plug protruding. After the

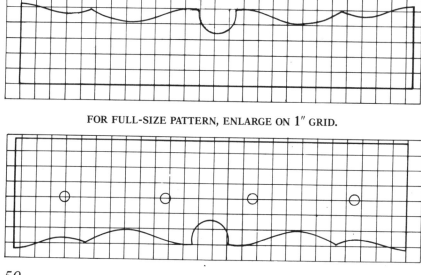

FOR FULL-SIZE PATTERN, ENLARGE ON 1″ GRID.

Illus. 11.2   Pattern for top board.

Illus. 11.3   Pattern for bottom board, showing location of coat hanger pegs.

Illus. 11.4   Counterbored holes in side. Start assembly with the top board and work down.

glue dries, sand the plugs flush. Check all of the surfaces for smoothness, and do additional sanding where needed.

Drawer Assembly

Saw parts for making the drawer box (Illus. 11.5). Cut a ¼″ dado ¼″ deep in each part to accommodate the plywood bottom (Illus.

Illus. 11.6   Drawer box, showing plywood bottom in place in dadoes.

11.6). Cut the drawer front and attach it to the assembled drawer box with screws driven from the back side (Illus. 11.7).

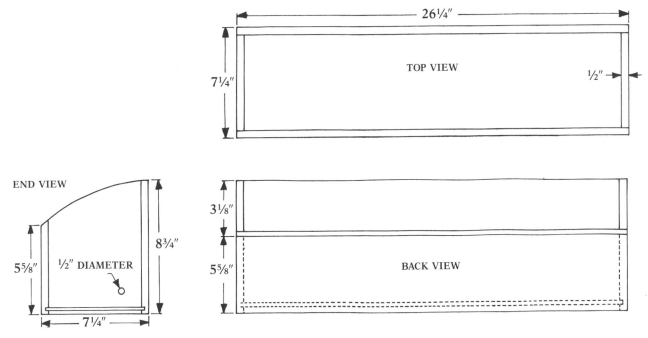

TOP VIEW

26¼″

7¼″

½″

END VIEW

½″ DIAMETER

8¾″

5⅝″

7¼″

BACK VIEW

3⅛″

5⅝″

Illus. 11.5   Drawer box dimensions.

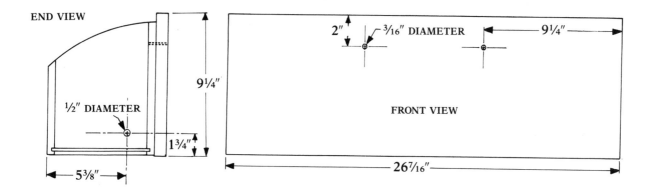

Illus. 11.7   Drawer front dimensions, showing its mounting to the drawer box.

Using a wood lathe, turn the coat hanger pegs (Illus. 11.8) and the drawer handle (Illus. 11.9). Note: factory-made pegs and handles are available at most hardware or lumber suppliers and may be used in place of the hand-turned parts.

Mounting the Drawer

The swing-down drawer is secured between the sides and under the bottom shelf with ½" dowel pins through both the shelf sides and the drawer end. To match the dowel holes so the dowel pins will fit through, secure the drawer in place temporarily while a ½" hole is drilled through the side and drawer end. Drive a ½"-diameter dowel pin into the hole to se-

cure the drawer. Repeat the procedures at the other side. Drive the ends of the dowel pins below the surface of the sides to allow a wood button to be placed over each. Do not glue the buttons so that the swing-down drawer can be removed if the need arises.

Glue the coat hanger pegs in the holes that were previously drilled in the bottom board. Attach the drawer handle.

Finishing

Apply stain as desired, following the manufacturer's directions. After the last application of stain is dry, apply polyurethane finish and sand with 220-grit paper between coats or, preferably, use 0000 steel wool.

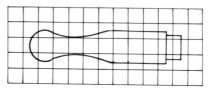

Illus. 11.8   Pattern for coat hanger peg.

FOR FULL-SIZE PATTERN, ENLARGE ON ½" GRID.

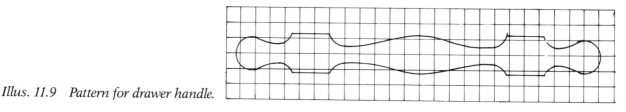

Illus. 11.9   Pattern for drawer handle.

Turned-Wood Table Accents

12 ◆ TURNED VASE

Turning items on your lathe may offer you the greatest opportunity to explore your creativity and at the same time produce practical objects for your home or as gifts. Another advantage of using the lathe is that you can effectively—and sometimes dramatically—utilize scraps of beautiful hardwoods that you just couldn't discard. The vase pictured was cut from cedar, walnut, and maple.

SUPPLIES

- Wood glue
- Band saw
- Lathe
- Turning tool
- Calipers, inside and outside
- Garnet paper, 50, 80, 120, 180, and 220 grit
- Drill, with ¾" bit
- Cloth for finishing
- Polyurethane finish

Materials		Quantity
Cedar	1⅞" × 5" × 5"	1
Cedar	1" × 5" × 5"	1
Maple	½" × 5" × 5"	2
Walnut	¾" × 5" × 5"	1

INSTRUCTIONS

The turning process is simple and straightforward, especially to anyone who has had previous opportunities to use the lathe. A block is glued up and cut to rough shape. The piece is turned and finishing is done in most cases right on the lathe, with slight touch-ups after. Before starting refer to the instructions for the following projects, numbers 13 and 14. Some of those instructions may be helpful here also.

Basic Cutting

Select your wood and glue up (Illus. 12.1). Square the ends, then scribe a circle on one end. Using a band saw and the circle as a guide, cut a cylinder from the wood.

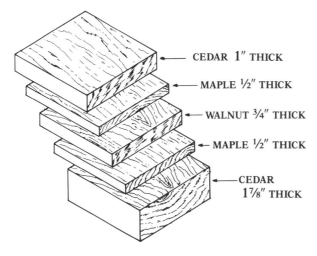

CEDAR 1" THICK

MAPLE ½" THICK

WALNUT ¾" THICK

MAPLE ½" THICK

CEDAR 1⅞" THICK

Illus. 12.1   Gluing up the wood for turning.

Illus. 12.2   Screw center on the right, faceplate on the left.

Preparing the Lathe

When working with a lathe it becomes important that the wood is held securely and latched down in place to prevent it from vibrating loose. When turning long cylindrical objects such as lamp stems, candlesticks, and ball bats, the work is held between two centers, one on the tail stock and the other on the head stock. The spur, which holds the wood causing it to turn, is also located at the headstock.

When shaping objects such as vases, bowls, lids, or round trays, the work is held with either a screw center or a faceplate (Illus. 12.2).

Turning to Shape

Secure a screw center to the lathe headstock, and attach the wood cylinder. Adjust the tool rest close to the work and to hold the cutting edge of the turning tool on center. Set the lathe on a slower speed and turn the work by hand to check for clearance. Turn the power on and cut the cylindrical stock down until it is perfectly round. Set the lathe on a higher speed, and turn the outside of the vase to the shape according to the pattern (Illus. 12.3). Adjust the tool rest to cut the top section of the vase cavity. Sand the piece smooth.

Finishing on the Lathe

Cut a six-inch square of cloth, and fold it several times to make a small pad. Dip one edge in clear polyurethane varnish, and hold it against the spinning wood, moving it back and forth sideways. Repeat the procedure until the entire surface is well covered with the finish. Continue to burnish the finish by holding the pad against the spinning vase. Allow the lathe to continue running for several minutes to aid the drying process.

It might be necessary to leave the screw center attached to the vase overnight to allow the finish to completely dry, otherwise it might be damaged as it is removed. After the finish is completely dry, remove the screw center, and saw the waste stock from the base.

Sand the base smooth.

Vase Cavity

Drill a ¾" hole from the top of the vase down the center to the depth shown in the pattern (Illus. 12.3).

1 SQUARE = ½ INCH SQUARE

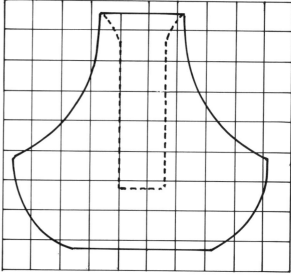

FOR FULL-SIZE PATTERN, ENLARGE ON ½" GRID.

Illus. 12.3   Turning pattern for vase, showing the vase cavity in dotted lines. Drill to the depth indicated.

13 ◆ TURNED FRUIT BOWL

Useful wood bowls of many sizes can bring just the right touch to your dining table and kitchen, or to any other part of your home. A beautiful bowl turned on your own lathe will have an extra special place in any home. The fruit bowl pictured is made of cedar, but you can turn it in almost any nontoxic wood.

SUPPLIES

- Wood glue
- Band saw
- Lathe
- Round nose tool
- Parting tool
- Skew chisel
- Calipers, inside and outside
- Garnet paper, 50, 80, 120, 180, and
    220 grit
- Cloth for finishing
- Polyurethane varnish

MATERIALS

Cedar, or wood or your choice: Solid, or
  glued up
Sufficient starting material for: 8″ diameter
  × 5″ height

INSTRUCTIONS

The glued up block is cut to rough shape and then attached with a faceplate. Before starting refer to the instructions for the previous project, number 12, the turned vase, which opens this group of projects on turned wood. Some of those instructions may be helpful here also.

Basic Cutting

Draw the full-size profile of the bowl on paper (Illus. 13.1). Glue up wood stock to provide enough thickness for the height of the project.

Cut a cylinder from the wood about ¼″ larger than the bowl diameter. The grain should run perpendicular to the cylinder sides. Center the lathe faceplate inside the circle on one end and attach it with screws. Screw the faceplate on the headstock. Adjust the tool rest close to the work and to hold the cutting edge of the tool on center.

Perfect Rounding on the Lathe

Set the lathe on slow speed and turn the work by hand to check for clearance. Turn the power on and cut the stock down until it is perfectly round. Roundness may be checked while the work is turning by holding the tool handle against the spinning wood. If the work is round, the handle will rub against the wood smoothly, if not it will feel bumpy and make a knocking noise.

Turning the Cavity to Shape

Move the tool rest out in front of the work. Again, check for clearance by turning the work by hand. Change the lathe to medium speed. First, true up the front surface, then start cutting the bowl cavity with a round nose tool. As the depth of the cavity permits, adjust the rest with one end extending inside the bowl cavity to support the tool. Move the rest often to provide maximum support to the tool. Special tool rests for turning bowls are available but the standard rest may be used for many bowl turning jobs. Shape the inside of the bowl to the desired shape, then sand with garnet paper, using progressively finer grits during the sanding operation.

Shaping the Outside

Move the tool rest back to the side position and shape the outside of the bowl. First, make a cut into the wood with a parting tool at the base of the the bowl. Rough out the shape with a round nose tool, then do the finish shaping by making fine cuts with the skew chisel and the round nose tool. Sand the outside at high speed on the lathe, using progressively finer grits, until smooth.

Finishing on the Lathe

Follow the instructions given for the previous project, number 12, the turned vase.

1 SQUARE = ½ INCH SQUARE

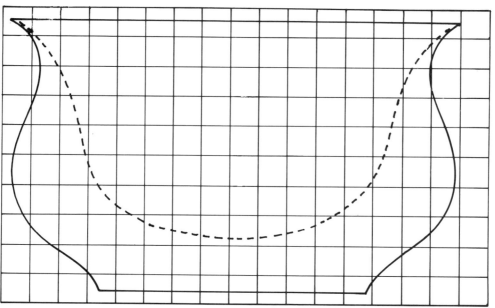

FOR FULL-SIZE PATTERN, ENLARGE ON 1″ GRID.

Illus. 13.1   Turning pattern for fruit bowl, showing the bowl cavity in dotted lines.

14 ◆ TURNED JAR LIDS

Handsomely finished turned wood lids seem to demonstrate the elegance of simplicity in the way they transform an ordinary glass jar into a treasure. Three sizes and styles are pictured, and you can adapt the small jar lid plan given to create the appropriate lids for your jars.

SUPPLIES

- Wood glue
- Saw
- Lathe
- Turning tools
- Calipers, inside and outside
- Garnet paper, 50, 80, 120, 180, 220
- Cloth for finishing
- Polyurethane varnish

MATERIALS

Hardwoods of your choice: Solid, or glued up
Pattern given requires: 2¼″ diameter × 2″ high

INSTRUCTIONS

The design presented is for a 2¼″ diameter jar lid made of laminated hardwoods. Use the other lids pictured to come up with variations. Execute each lid design following the same basic instructions, while also referring to earlier turning projects, numbers 12 and 13, to supplement these instructions.

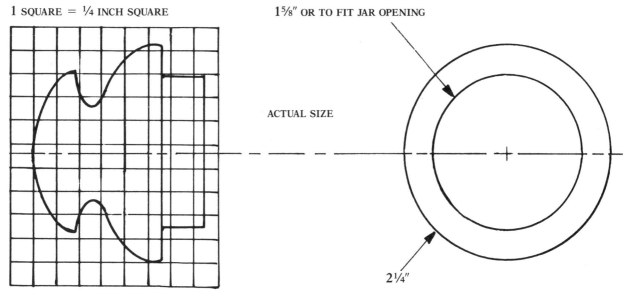

1 SQUARE = ¼ INCH SQUARE

1⅝″ OR TO FIT JAR OPENING

ACTUAL SIZE

2¼″

Illus. 14.1   Turning pattern for laminated jar lid, with view of lid bottom for jar fitting.

Basic Cutting

Draw the outline shape of the pattern full-size on paper (Illus. 14.1). Cut the wood stock to rough shape and drill a small pilot hole about one inch deep in the center of one end.

Turning on the Lathe

Screw the wood on the center securely. Set the tool rest close to the work and at a height which will hold the tool cutting edge on center. Turn the work by hand to check for clearance and make sure the work is secured. Set the lathe on medium speed. Use a gouge to cut the wood down to be concentric. Transfer the measurements from the paper pattern to the wood. Mark high and low cuts with a pencil.

Using a round nose tool and a skew chisel, turn the wood to the general desired shape (Illus. 14.2). Do the final finish shaping of the lid by making fine cuts to work the wood gradually into shape.

Sanding on the Lathe

Set the lathe on fast speed. Sand the surface by moving garnet paper rapidly back and forth sideways on the spinning wood. Start with coarse grit garnet paper, changing to finer grits as the sanding progresses.

Illus. 14.2 An example of cutting to general shape, using a skew chisel on stock screwed to a faceplate.

Finishing on the Lathe

Apply finish as described for the turned vase, project number 12, which opens this group of projects on turned wood.

15 ◆ TURNED LAMP

Lamps add mood and warmth to a room, and turning your own lamp offers a chance to express your own creativity in your decor. The lamp pictured is glued up from stock of solid walnut. Besides strengthening the piece, the gluing-up process results in an intricate design of various grains and textures.

SUPPLIES

- Plane
- Table saw
- Carpenter's glue
- "C" clamps
- Mallet
- Center punch or large nail
- Lathe with turning tools
- Sandpaper in coarse, medium, and fine grits
- Drill with 7/16", 5/16", and 1½" drill bits
- Polyurethane finish
- 000 steel wool

Materials		Quantity
Walnut boards	13/16" × 3½" × 18"	8
Lamp hardware:	3/8" pipe cut to 7" length	
	1 hexagonal nut	
	1 knurled nut	
	harp, shade, and finial	
	cord and lamp socket	

INSTRUCTIONS

Follow the pattern given (Illus. 15.1). The lamp base is large enough to accommodate a harp for holding the lamp shade. Smaller bases may also be turned using the same pattern by simply reducing it by the desired amount. A smaller base will result in a fine bedside light, using a clip-on shade.

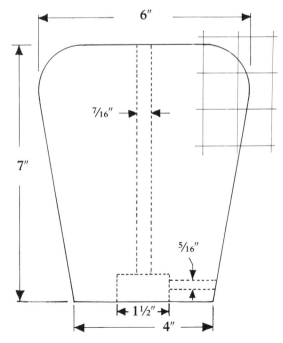

Illus. 15.1   Pattern for lamp base, showing locations of holes.

59

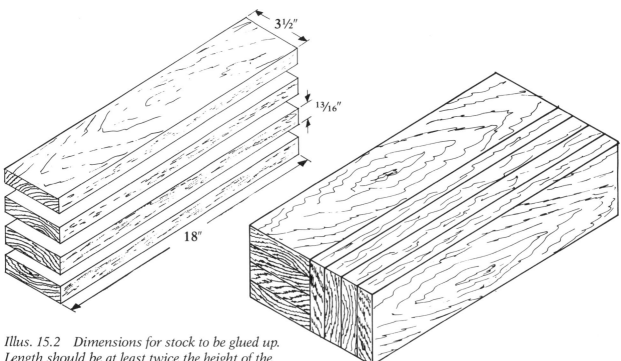

Illus. 15.2   Dimensions for stock to be glued up. Length should be at least twice the height of the lamp base plus sufficient room to work on the lathe.

Illus. 15.3   Two groups of boards glued together with end grain at 90° to each other.

Basic Cutting

Plane lumber to ¹³⁄₁₆″ thickness, then rip to the specified width (Illus. 15.2). Cut eight boards 16 inches long. These are twice the rough height of the glued-up starting block. The boards are assembled in steps and then cut in half.

Gluing up the Block

Separate the boards into two groups of four each. Arrange and stack the boards in each group in the order in which they are to be glued. Spread a coating of glue on the boards one joint at a time, stacking them in the prearranged order. Apply a "C" clamp at each end of the stacked group of boards. Working alternately from clamp to clamp, gradually tighten clamps while at the same time keeping the boards aligned by tapping them in place with a mallet. After the two clamps have been tightened enough to hold them in place, apply pressure on both sides with additional clamps closely spaced.

Repeat these procedures in gluing up the second stack of boards. After the glue dries, plane the glued-up stock to true up all sides. Glue the two groups of boards together with end grain running at 90 degrees to each other (Illus. 15.3). After glue between these two groups dries, cut them into equal lengths and glue as shown in (Illus. 15.4).

Preparing the Block for Turning

Using a table saw, cut the four corners off at 45 degrees to form an octagon. This will make the stock more nearly round and easier to turn on the lathe. Locate center of each end by drawing lines across from opposite corners. Using a center punch or large nail, tap a hole at center on each end. Remove both centers from lathe. Seat them in the ends of wood stock by tapping them with a mallet. Secure wood stock between lathe centers and adjust tool rest. Lock the tail stock and tool rest in place.

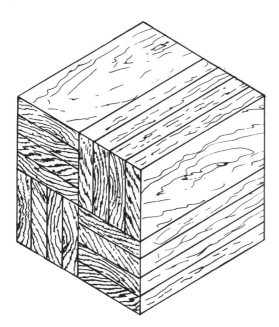

Illus. 15.4   Block formed by cutting glued-up groups into equal lengths and then gluing the halves to form working stock for lathe.

Turning to Shape

Turn the wood by hand to check for clearance. Set lathe on slowest speed to make first cut. Increase the speed after the stock has been rounded. Turn the wood to the shape of the pattern, stopping the lathe frequently to check progress.

Sanding on the Lathe

Set the lathe speed on fast while sanding. Keep the sandpaper moving sideways to prevent deep scratches. Start with coarse or medium grit garnet paper, and use progressively finer grits as the sanding progresses. Stop the lathe and sand with the grain to remove small scratches.

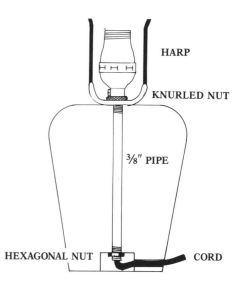

Illus. 15.5   Assembly of lamp parts.

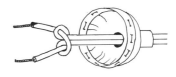

Illus. 15.6   Underwriter's Laboratories' knot used to secure cord in socket base.

Lamp Assembly and Finishing

Bore holes in the base as indicated in the pattern. Apply polyurethane finish as desired. Slide the ⅜" pipe in place with a hexagonal nut on its lower end (Illus. 15.5). Secure the base for the harp using a knurled nut. Thread the cord through the pipe and loose socket base. Tie the Underwriter Laboratories' Knot (Illus. 15.6) and follow manufacturer's directions to complete lamp assembly.

16 ◆ CANDLE STAND

Materials		Quantity
Stem	$2'' \times 2'' \times 10''$	1
Tray	$1\frac{1}{2}'' \times 8\frac{1}{2}'' \times 8\frac{1}{2}''$	1
Base	$2'' \times 7'' \times 7''$	1

SUPPLIES

- Saw
- Pencil and chalk
- Mallet
- Transfer paper
- Lathe with turning tools
- Sandpaper of various grits
- Small cloth for finishing
- Linseed oil, with shellac or varnish

This turned walnut stand makes a perfect holiday decoration. A large cylindrical candle can be placed for festive dinner celebrations or for a quiet holiday mood. The tray that supports the candle is large enough so that this piece can double as a candy tray.

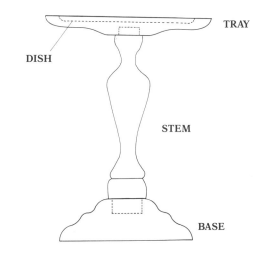

Illus. 16.1   Candle stand assembly, showing the three elements that must be turned separately.

INSTRUCTIONS

You should have some prior experience with your lathe before turning this project. The piece requires four completely separate turning operations, and each section has to balance and fit properly with the other elements (Illus. 16.1). The stem (Illus. 16.2) is a straightforward turning operation. The tray (Illus. 16.3), however, requires two separate operations to turn the dish side of the tray and the underside. The final element, the base (Illus. 16.4), requires only one turning operation.

Basic Cutting

Enlarge the patterns to full size. Cut the wood stock to size for the stem, the tray, and the base, according to the dimensions given in the materials list. Allow about an inch extra for the stem for chucking in the lathe.

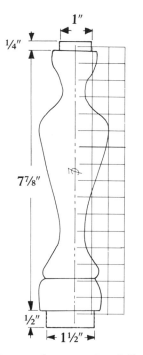

Illus. 16.2 Pattern for stem. For full-size pattern, enlarge on a ½" grid.

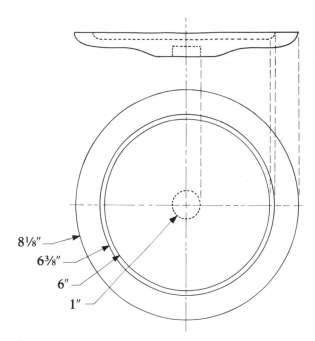

Illus. 16.3 Pattern for tray.

Turning the Stem

Find the center at each end by drawing diagonal lines from corner to corner. Cut grooves with a saw or wide chisel to help seat the headstock spur (Illus. 16.5). Use a mallet to tap the centers into the wood stock.

Secure the wood stock between lathe centers and adjust the tool rest. Lock the tail stock and tool rest in place, then turn the wood by hand to make sure it clears.

Set the lathe speed on slow to make the first cut. Increase the speed after the stock has been rounded.

Transfer the design of the full-size pattern by measuring and marking high and low places (Illus. 16.6). Stop the lathe frequently and check diameters and to make sure the wood is held securely between centers. The tool rest should also be adjusted often as the diameter of the wood decreases (Illus. 16-7).

Sanding the Stem

Set the lathe speed fast while sanding the project. Keep the sandpaper moving sideways to prevent deep scratches. Start with coarse or

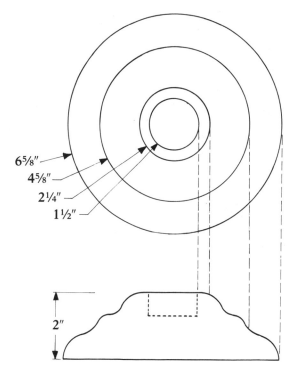

Illus. 16.4 Pattern for base.

medium grit garnet paper, using finer grits as the sanding progresses. For the final sanding step, stop the lathe and sand with the grain to remove small scratches.

Illus. 16.5   Seating the headstock spur in the starting piece for the stem.

Illus. 16.6   Marking design on rounded stock.

Illus. 16.7   Adjust the tool shelf for decreasing diameter of wood.

Finishing

A linseed oil, or combination with shellac or varnish, finish may be applied to the turned pieces as a final step.

Fold a small cloth several times to form a pad. Apply the finish to the pad, then hold the pad against the revolving wood. Apply the finish in several light coats, burnishing each coat by applying light pressure to the pad as it is moved back and forth across the project. Continue applying the finish until the desired sheen is obtained.

Making the Tray

Two separate turning operations are required to make the tray (Illus. 16.8). The first operation is the turning of the dish side of the tray (Illus. 16.9). After turning the dish shape, remove the faceplate and attach it to the opposite side inside the dish shape just turned (Illus. 16.10).

To prepare the stock for turning, scribe a circle about ½" larger in diameter than the finished piece. This will allow ½" removal of material during the turning process.

Set the lathe on the lowest speed and adjust the tool rest to do cutting on the outside diameter of the disc to true it up. Do not, at this time, attempt to do any shaping of the outside perimeter other than to true it up. True up the front surface of the material. Using a pencil, measure and mark the diameter of the dish shape to be turned. Increase the lathe speed and proceed to cut the dish shape to size.

Remove the faceplate from the wood and attach it to the opposite side, making sure it is centered as nearly as possible. Turn the underside of the tray to the desired shape. Screw the faceplate back on the headstock and true up the outside edge. Apply finish as described above for the stem.

Turning the Base and Assembly

Proceed in turning the base in the same manner as the bottom of the dish was turned. Apply finish as described above for the stem. Assemble the stem, tray, and base with glue, or leave unglued for later disassembly.

Clockwise from upper left:
Planter Cart; Adirondack Chair;
Mug Rack; Dulcimer; Stencilled
Flower Box.

A

*Clockwise from upper left:
Doll Cradle; Bookends;
Telephone Shelf; Turned
Jar Lids; Holiday Sleigh.*

Clockwise from upper left: Candle Stand; Hardwood Stool; Desk Trays; Baseball Card Case; Pie Safe.

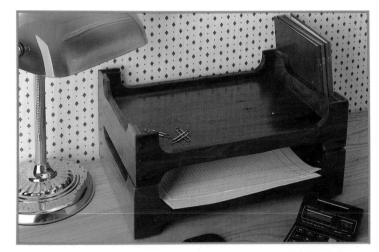

Clockwise from upper left: Apothecary Case; Napkin Holder; Turned Fruit Bowl; Turned Lamp; Deacon's Bench.

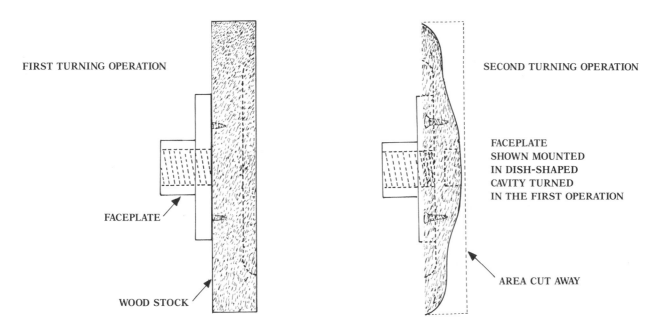

FIRST TURNING OPERATION

SECOND TURNING OPERATION

FACEPLATE
SHOWN MOUNTED
IN DISH-SHAPED
CAVITY TURNED
IN THE FIRST OPERATION

FACEPLATE

AREA CUT AWAY

WOOD STOCK

Illus. 16.8   Separate turning operations required for the tray.

Illus. 16.9   Turning the dish side of the tray.

Illus. 16.10   Faceplate reattached to the dish shape just turned.

17 ◆ MANTEL CLOCK

This handsome clock is simple to construct. The scroll design of the top combines with the turned columns to give the piece a vintage look. The turning is straightforward, only requiring one turning operation that can be adapted to suit your own design ideas. The turned piece is then sawn in half to give identical "pillars."

MATERIALS

- Walnut and other wood
- Single-strength glass, for front
- Hinges
- Latch
- Clock movement

SUPPLIES

- Table saw
- Router, with Roman ogee bit
- Wood glue
- Screws
- Finishing nails
- Clamps
- Lathe, with turning tools
- Drill
- Sandpaper, in various grits
- Varnish

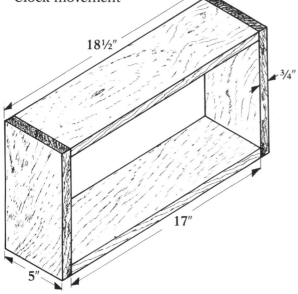

Illus. 17.1   Basic box construction on the mantel clock.

INSTRUCTIONS

The construction of this clock is basically a 9½" by 18½" box without bottom or top (Illus. 17.1). Other elements of the design are added to provide a battery-powered mantel clock with an antique appearance (Illus. 17.2).

Basic Cutting

Assemble all materials needed and enlarge the pattern of the scroll design, which will be fastened to the top (Illus. 17.3).

Rip materials to proper widths according to working drawings.

Cut parts to length.

Box Assembly

Assemble the box (Illus. 17.1). Counterbore ⅜″ holes about halfway through the end boards for screwheads, then drill holes through the remaining half to fit screw shank (Illus. 17.4).

Attach end boards to the sides with glue and screws. After glue dries, sand joints and plugged holes flush with surrounding wood.

Front Assembly

Assemble front of the clock with glue and clamps (Illus. 17.5). Sand joints flush.

Secure the front to box with glue and clamps. Small finishing nails might be driven through the ends of the front to hold it in place while it is being clamped. The nails will be covered with corner boards.

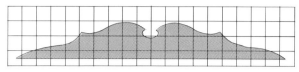

Illus. 17.3   Scroll design pattern for top piece. For full-size pattern, enlarge on grid with 1″ squares.

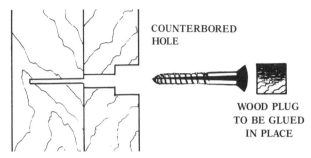

COUNTERBORED HOLE

WOOD PLUG TO BE GLUED IN PLACE

Illus. 17.4   Counterboring and covering screws with wood plugs.

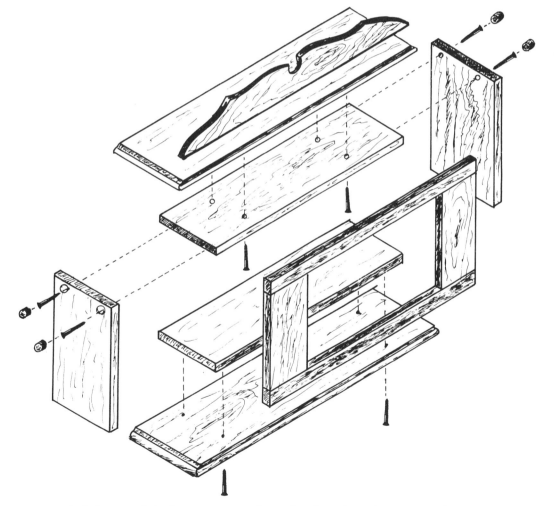

Illus. 17.2   Exploded view of clock structure, without the glass door, decorative columns, or movement.

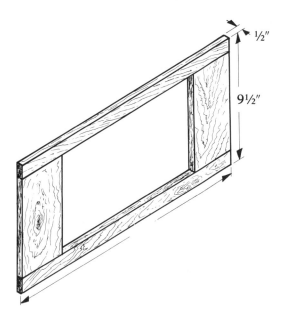

Illus. 17.5   Front assembly.

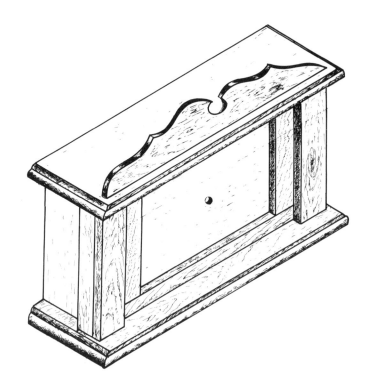

Illus. 17.7   Basic clock structure, without the glass door, decorative columns, or movement.

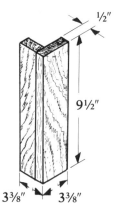

Illus. 17.6   Dimensions for corner boards.

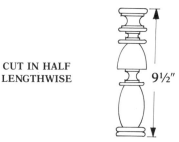

CUT IN HALF
LENGTHWISE

Illus. 17.8   Length and shape for turned ornamental post.

Assemble corner boards (Illus. 17.6) with glue and clamps, or with glue and small screws. If screws are used, they should be plugged (Illus. 17.4). After the glue dries, sand surfaces flush. Attach corner boards to front corners of the clock.

Top and Bottom Boards, and Scroll Design

Sand top and bottom boards, then rout ends and sides with Roman ogee router bit. Saw scroll-design top piece (Illus. 17.3) to shape and sand. Attach this top ornament to top board with screws driven from the bottom.

Secure the bottom board and top board with ornament onto the box to form the basic clock structure (Illus. 17.7).

Turning the Ornamental Post

Turn the ornamental post on a lathe (Illus. 17.8). The length is fixed, but the shape can be varied to suit your own sense of design. Cut the ornamental post in half lengthwise to form two halves. Mount these halves on the corner boards (Illus. 17.9).

Illus. 17.9   Half of turned ornamental post mounted on front corner boards.

Clock Face and Glass Door

Make the clock face which is to be mounted from back side to cover opening. Drill a hole in the middle to accommodate the shank of clock. Make the door frame that will hold the front glass piece (Illus. 17.10).

Finishing

Apply finish to all wood parts following the manufacturer's directions.

Installing Clock Movement

Install clock works according to the manufacturer's suggested methods. This will originally involve a simple operation of placing the clock shank through the hole, then securing with a washer and nut. Clock hands are then attached.

Attach numerals to the clock face according to accompanying instructions. Some numerals are self-adhering and are simply pressed firmly in place.

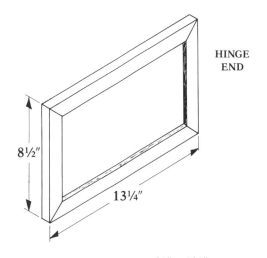

HINGE END

8½"

13¼"

MADE FROM ¾" × 1⅛" MATERIAL

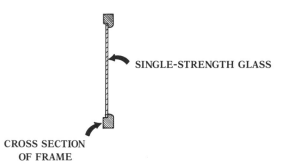

SINGLE-STRENGTH GLASS

CROSS SECTION OF FRAME

Illus. 17.10   Door frame for glass cover, with cross section showing glass placement.

Install glass in door frame (Illus. 17.10). Attach the glass door to the clock with small hinges and latch.

Display and Decorative Accessories

18 ◆ DULCIMER

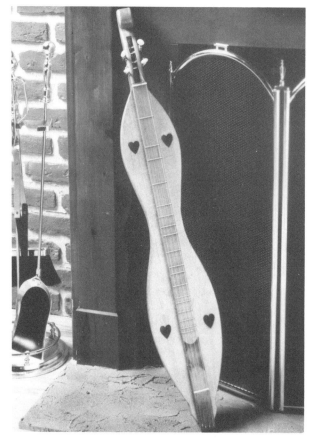

You will always want to keep this instrument on display, whether or not you want to play it. The Appalachian Mountain origin of the dulcimer gives this simple, graceful instrument a charm and elegance worthy of any home, not just in the country. The name means "sweet sound" and was probably borrowed from the older hammered dulcimer popular in different parts of Europe. In some areas the Appalachian dulcimer is called a hog fiddle.

INSTRUCTIONS

The dulcimer pictured features a spruce soundboard with the other parts being maple or walnut stained in Provincial and Colonial maple. The instrument has a central fingerboard that supports the soundboard in two halves over the sound box. At one end is a peg box for tuning the four strings. The only unusual tool required, a heated drum for bending the wood for the sides, is actually simple to construct from a piece of metal pipe and a propane torch.

SUPPLIES

- Twelve ¾" wire brads
- Carpenter's glue
- Band saw
- Plane
- Drill, with ¼" and ¹⁄₁₆" bits
- Wood file
- Router
- Sander
- Hot glue gun
- Utility knife

- Carving tools or lathe (for pegs)
- Violin peg hole reamer and peg shaver
- Sponge or tub of water
- Heated drum, propane torch in stainless steel or copper pipe
- "C" clamps and spool clamps, if available
- Plywood block and sandpaper
- Wood stain, Provincial and Colonial maple
- Semi-gloss polyurethane, spray
- 000 steel wool

Materials			Quantity
Maple or walnut:	Peg box	$1\frac{3}{4}'' \times 3\frac{1}{4}'' \times 9\frac{1}{2}''$	1
	End block	$1\frac{3}{4}'' \times 3\frac{1}{2}'' \times 2\frac{1}{2}''$	1
	Fingerboard	$\frac{3}{4}'' \times 1\frac{3}{4}'' \times 32''$	1
	Pegs	$1'' \times 1'' \times 4''$	4
Spruce:	Soundboard	$1\frac{1}{8}'' \times 4\frac{1}{2}'' \times 32''$	2
Maple:	Sides	$\frac{1}{8}'' \times 1\frac{3}{4}'' \times 32''$	2
	Back	$\frac{1}{8}'' \times 9'' \times 32''$	1
Instrument hardware:	nut		1
	bridge		1
	string anchors		4
	set of strings		1

Making the Peg Box

Enlarge pattern to full size (Illus. 18.1). Plane wood to specified thickness. Cut a 7″ by 19″ block from the planed lumber. Cut a ¾″ groove halfway down the length of the board in the middle of one edge (Illus. 18.2). Transfer pattern of peg box to wood with its top edge aligned with the top edge of the board. Cut peg box to shape with a band saw.

Lay out and cut grooves in the sides with the band saw (Illus. 18.3). Glue wedges to the peg box with hot glue gun. Mark the locations of the peg holes and drill through the block with a ¼″ drill. Taper each hole using a violin peg-hole reamer. Finish shaping the peg box using a wood file and sander. A router might be used to round some of the edges. Fine-sand all surfaces after shaping has been completed.

Illus. 18.2   Groove being cut in block from which the peg box will be made. The groove will become the hollow for attaching strings to pegs.

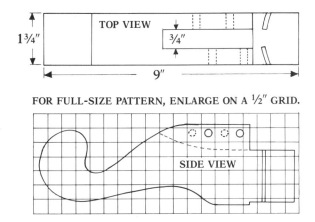

TOP VIEW

1¾″

¾″

9″

FOR FULL-SIZE PATTERN, ENLARGE ON A ½″ GRID.

SIDE VIEW

Illus. 18.1   Pattern for peg box.

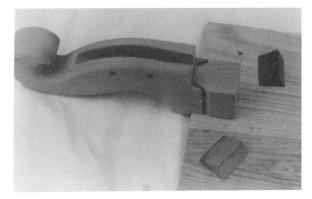

Illus. 18.3   Peg box with wedges ready to be attached.

Making the End Block

Enlarge pattern to full size (Illus. 18.4). Plane the wood to the specified thickness, then transfer the pattern to the wood. Cut to shape with a band saw. Lay out and cut grooves for attaching the sides (Illus. 18.5). Sand the edges smooth.

The Fingerboard

First, rip materials to specified width, then cut to length (Illus. 18.6). Cut the thumping hollow with a band saw and sand to shape. Cut a hollow in the back side of fingerboard by running a groove to either side of the thumping hollow.

Cut grooves across top side to accommodate the nut and bridge. The total distance between the nut and bridge is called the scale length. The position of fret grooves is calculated as follows. To establish the location of the first fret down from the nut, divide the scale length by 17.835. Mark this distance down from the nut. For the scale length of the second fret down, subtract the distance of the first fret from the scale length and divide the remainder by 17.835. For the third fret, subtract the distance between the first and second fret from the remainder, and again divide by 17.835. Continue in this manner to establish all of the fret locations. Some frets are left out on the dulcimer fingerboard (compare your calculated frets to Illus. 18.6), but these can simply be erased after all have been marked. If you prefer, you can purchase a ready-made fingerboard, complete with frets and the hollow cut in the back side, available from many supply houses.

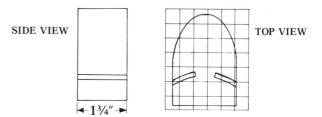

SIDE VIEW   TOP VIEW

←1¾″→

Illus. 18.4   Pattern for end block. For full-size pattern, enlarge on a ½″ grid.

Illus. 18.5   Completed end block with grooves to accommodate sides.

The Soundboard and Back

The soundboard is made in two halves, each half being 4½″ wide. Attach the two halves of the soundboard to the bottom side of the fingerboard, leaving the hollow open down the middle (Illus. 18.7). Cut a pattern of the dulcimer body shape from heavy paper and center it over the soundboard asembly and trace around it (Illus. 18.8). Transfer the same pat-

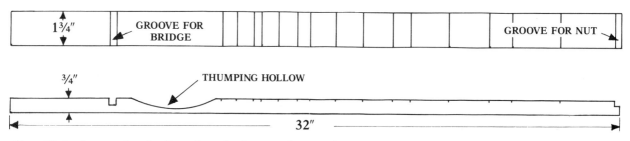

1¾″   GROOVE FOR BRIDGE   GROOVE FOR NUT

¾″   THUMPING HOLLOW

32″

Illus. 18.6   Layout for the fingerboard, showing frets and grooves. Don't rely on the drawing; calculate the fret locations as described in the text to achieve the highest degree of exactness.

72

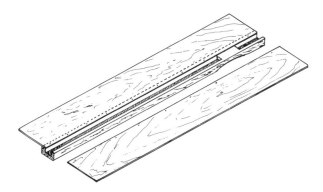

Illus. 18.7   Halves of the soundboard being attached to the back of the fingerboard, leaving the groove uncovered.

Rock the wood from side to side as you press it against the heated drum. The rocking motion not only helps form a smooth curve but prevents wood from scorching. Start the bending process at the large curve at the middle of the side. Check the progress of the bending process often by placing it over the pattern for comparison. After both sides are shaped, allow them to dry.

tern to the bottom board, then rough-cut both the soundboard and the back to shape. Cut about ¼″ outside of the lines of the pattern using a sharp utility knife. Cut the sound holes in the soundboard.

Bending the Sides

Rip the side material to width. The width should be the same as the thickness of the end block and peg box extension where grooves are cut for attaching sides. The sides are bent to shape by applying moisture with a sponge or by soaking. Hard close-grain woods require soaking.

Press the moisture-laden sides against a heated drum (Illus. 18.9). The drum is made from a stainless steel or copper pipe heated with a propane torch. The torch blows heat inside the pipe, which is closed at one end.

Illus. 18.9   Bending the dulcimer sides to shape by pressing the moisture-laden wood over a heated drum.

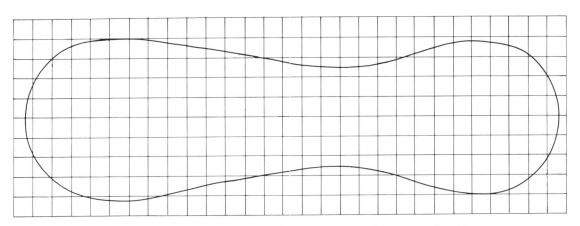

Illus. 18.8   Pattern for dulcimer body shape. For full-size pattern, enlarge on a 1″ grid.

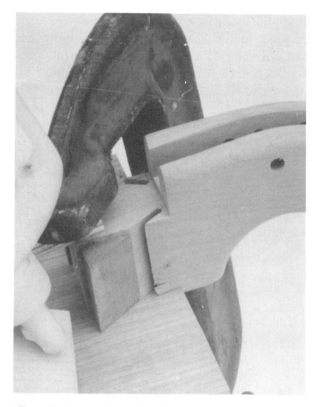

Illus. 18.10 Side and peg box assembly, showing clamp arrangement and glue being applied to side.

Assembling the Sides

Clamp the peg box to a board, and then, using glue, secure the ends of the sides in the grooves (Illus. 18.10). Glue the opposite ends of the sides in the grooves which have been cut in end block (Illus. 18.11). Using spacers on the inside and boards clamped to press against the outside, mould and secure the sides to the shape of the dulcimer body pattern. Clamp the end block and the peg box in place with "C" clamps and allow the glue to dry (Illus. 18.12).

Assembling the Soundboard to the Sides

Align the soundboard on top of the sides with the fingerboard pressed against the peg box. Check to make sure of a close fit all around. If the sides need sanding, use a plywood block large enough to accommodate a full sheet of sandpaper, and sand across both sides at the same time to prevent sanding low places in the sides. Once the sides and soundboard fit prop-

Illus. 18.11 Sides and end block assembly.

erly, apply carpenter's glue to the top edges of the sides and again align the soundboard on top. Clamp with "C" clamps by placing a board on each side of the fingerboard to protect more evenly. Spool-type clamps can also be used.

Attaching the Back

Align the back on the sides and check for proper fit as was done with the soundboard. Apply glue to the edges of the sides, then clamp with "C" clamps and protect bottom or soundboard from damage by placing other boards between clamps and these parts. Spool-type clamps can also be used. Use a layer of cork glued to each disc of the spool clamps to prevent marring the dulcimer. After the glue dries, trim excess wood from the soundboard and the back. Leave the last ⅛" to be sanded. After the soundboard and the back have been sanded to shape, fine-sand all surfaces where needed.

Placing String Anchors

Lay out the locations of string anchors, making sure they coincide with those of the nut and bridge. One way to make sure is to lay out

Illus. 18.12   Glued-up side assembly clamped to dry. Spacer supports can be used along the inside to mould the body to the shape of the pattern. Boards can also be clamped along the outside to press the sides into the proper shape.

the nut or the bridge across the tail piece at the anchor locations, and then mark with a sharp tool or pencil. Drill a 1/16″ hole at each location. Drill each hole at an angle, tipping back to prevent string loops from slipping off. Tap the anchors in place, leaving about 3/16″ sticking up to hold the string loop.

Making Pegs

The pegs may be shaped by hand carving or by turning them out on a lathe. If turned on a lathe, the ball top can be flattened on each side to form the top of the peg. With either method, leave the peg stem larger than the peg holes to allow them to be tapered with a violin peg shaver. Drill string holes in the peg stems, then secure the pegs in the previously cut tapered holes in the peg box.

Finishing

After fine-sanding, remove all dust from the surfaces and apply Provincial stain. Wipe excess stain from surfaces, then apply a coat of Colonial maple stain, and again remove the excess. Allow stain to dry for eight hours, then apply three coats of semi-gloss polyurethane finish. Smooth between coats with 000 steel wool. Attach strings to the instrument.

19 ♦ HOLIDAY SLEIGH

This holiday sleigh is just the right size for a centerpiece or for showcasing your decorations on the mantel. You can build the sleigh from oak to finish or from easy-to-work-with pine to paint decoratively.

SUPPLIES

- Twenty 1″ wire brads and/or screws with wood plugs
- Carpenter's glue
- Carbon paper
- Garnet paper, 80, 100, and 150 grit
- Scroll saw
- Plane
- Drill, with a ³⁄₁₆″ drill bit
- Router, with a ¼″ rounding-over bit
- Half-round wood file (optional)
- Nail set
- Plastic wood or colored putty
- Finishing materials

INSTRUCTIONS

The construction is very straightforward. It is primarily a scroll saw project cut from ½″ material. The pieces are secured with glue and wire brads or screws. Depending on the wood you use, you can select whatever method of finishing fits in most with your holiday decor, including decorative painting.

Materials		Quantity
Runners	½″ × 6″ × 14″	2
Sleigh bottom	½″ × 2¾″ × 4¾″	1
Sleigh back	½″ × 2¾″ × 3¼″	1
Sides	½″ × 4″ × 8″	2
Seat	⅞″ × 1⅜″ × 2¾″	1
Dowel	³⁄₁₆″ × 4″	1

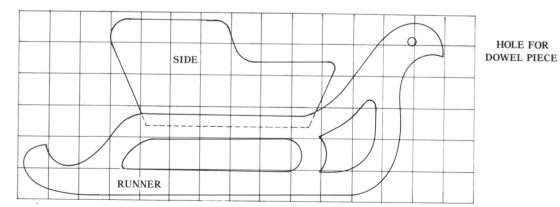

HOLE FOR
DOWEL PIECE

SIDE

RUNNER

Illus. 19.1   Pattern for runner and side of sleigh bed. For full-size pattern, enlarge on a 1″ grid.

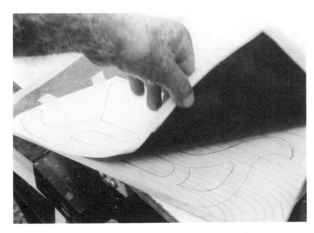

Illus. 19.2 Transferring pattern to wood with carbon paper.

Basic Cutting

Enlarge the patterns to full-size on 1″ grids (Illus. 19.1). Plane boards to ½″ thickness, then transfer the patterns of the runners and the sides of bed to the wood with carbon paper (Illus. 19.2). Saw out the traced parts with a scroll saw (Illus. 19.3). Cut the bottom, back, and seat to size (Illus. 19.4 and 19.5). Drill a ³⁄₁₆″ hole in the front of each runner as indicated on the pattern, then sand all surfaces, including edges, with medium-grit garnet paper. A half-round wood file will help smooth the inside cuts on the two runners but should be followed by sanding with medium-grit paper. Rout around all edges on the outer side of runners and bed sides with a ¼″ rounding-over bit.

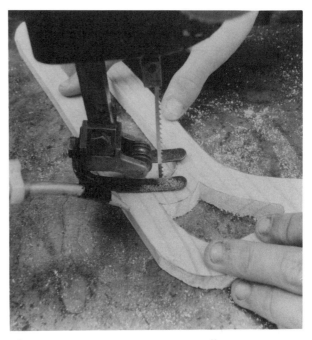

Illus. 19.3 Sawing runner on scroll saw.

Assembly

When using wire brads in the construction, you can avoid crushing the wood with the hammer by tapping the nails in only part way. Later, you can use a nail set to tap the nails flush or slightly below the surface if the nail head is to be covered with plastic wood or putty.

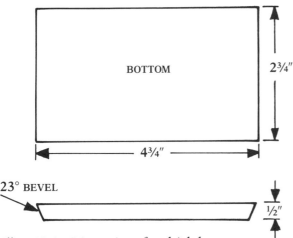

BOTTOM

2¾″

4¾″

23° BEVEL

½″

Illus. 19.4 Dimensions for sleigh bottom.

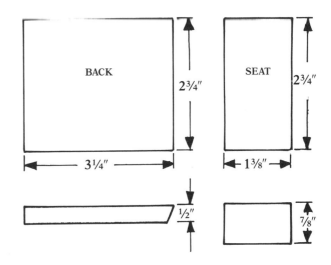

BACK

2¾″

3¼″

½″

SEAT

2¾″

1³⁄₈″

⅞″

Illus. 19.5 Dimensions for sleigh bed back and seat.

Illus. 19.6 *Nailing side to bottom.*

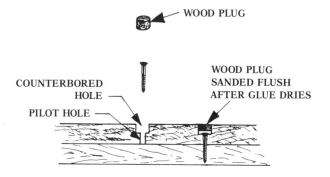

Illus. 19.8 *Counterboring and covering screws with wood plugs.*

WOOD PLUG

COUNTERBORED HOLE

PILOT HOLE

WOOD PLUG SANDED FLUSH AFTER GLUE DRIES

Illus. 19.7 *Fitting the back between the sides.*

Illus. 19.9 *Placing dowel through holes in front part of runners.*

Fasten the sides of the sleigh bed to the bottom with glue and 1″ wire brads (Illus. 19.6). Fit the back in place by sliding it between the two sides and down behind the bottom (Illus. 19.7). Fasten with 1″ wire brads.

The runners can be fastened to the assembled sleigh bed in either of two ways. Glue and 1″ wire brads will serve well if the sleigh is to be painted, but if stain and a clear finish is to be used, screws covered with wood plugs will serve better (Illus. 19.8).

Fit the ³⁄₁₆″ dowel through the holes in the front of runners (Illus. 19.9). Drive the heads of wire brads below the surface with a nail set (Illus. 19.10), then fill the holes with plastic wood or colored putty.

Illus. 19.10 *Setting wire brads with nail set.*

Finishing

Sand all surfaces with fine grit garnet paper, then apply finish as desired.

20 ♦ WINDMILL

This windmill can be displayed as a piece of collectible folk art or used as the center of decorations, especially with flowers. The Dutch association of windmills suggests the beautiful flowers of Holland. You can use cheery tulips, as pictured, and other floral designs to decorate the vanes and sides. The windmill actually turns and is easy to cut and assemble.

SUPPLIES

- Saw
- Router, with a ¼″ rounding-over bit
- Drill
- Two 1¼″ No. 8 hardboard screws
- Three 8d finishing nails
- Wood glue
- Sandpaper, in various grits
- Wood putty
- Finish or paint, as desired

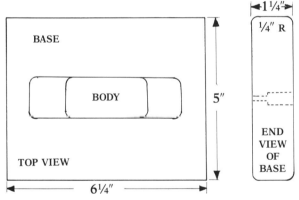

Illus. 20.1   Dimensions for windmill base, showing position and top and bottom outlines of windmill body.

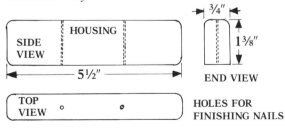
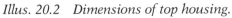

Illus. 20.2   Dimensions of top housing.

Materials	
Starting material:	
Body, base, and vanes	1¼″ × 6″ × 24″
Top housing and collar	¾″ × 6″ × 12″
Windmill hub	1″ × 1⁵⁄₁₆″ × 1⁵⁄₁₆″
Wooden bead	

INSTRUCTIONS

Dimensions are given for all of the parts except for the body, which can be gotten from the dimensions for the base (Illus. 20.1).

Basic Cutting

Cut parts to shape for the base and the body. Cut the top housing (Illus. 20.2) and the windmill collar to shape (Illus. 20.3). Rout around the edges as indicated (Illus. 20.4).

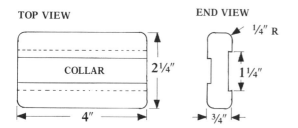

Illus. 20.3   Dimensions of windmill collar.

Illus. 20.4   Routing radius on edges of windmill body. A ¼" radius is routed on parts as indicated in drawings.

Cut the parts for the windmill vanes and the hub (Illus. 20.5).

Assembly

Refer to the side view and front view of the full assembly while you prepare the pieces and begin assembly (Illus. 20.6). Counterbore and drill pilot holes in the base. Drill pilot holes for nails in the top housing. Drill a hole to accommodate a finishing nail through the center of the windmill hub.

Sand all surfaces that will be exposed after assembly.

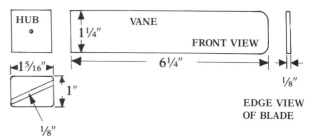

Illus. 20.5   Dimensions for windmill vanes and hub.

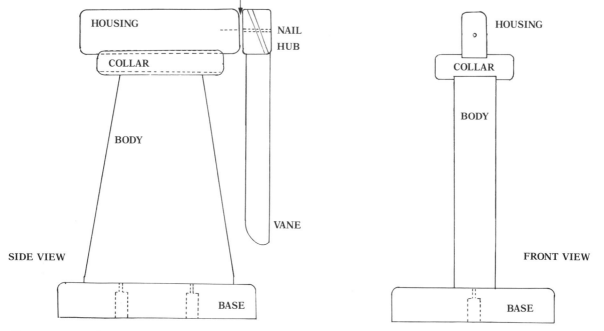

Illus. 20.6   Full assembly of the windmill.

Glue the windmill vanes to the hub, making sure that each vane is seated down on the bottom of the diagonal groove. Attach the base to the bottom with screws. Glue the collar and top housing in place, securing them with finishing nails. Set the nails below the surface using a nail set, then fill the holes with wood putty.

Attach the vane and hub assembly to the top housing with a nail, placing a wood bead between the hub and the housing to serve as a bearing (Illus. 20.7). Leave about ⅛″ of nail sticking out from the hub to allow the vanes to turn freely.

Finishing

Apply finish as desired. Your windmill is ready to be decorated with designs in paint, if you prefer.

Illus. 20.7   Bead between hub and housing serves as a bearing. Nail is left extended to allow blades to turn freely.

21 ✦ BASEBALL CARD CASE

A briefcase-style portable baseball card case will help fans and collectors keep their cards clean, damage-free, and neat. The design has four rows, allowing you to categorize dozens of cards. The walnut wood case features a latched lid that you can remove for convenient access when sorting or displaying cards on a table at a trade show. For other enthusiasts, a few modifications will turn the case into a storage, carrying, and display case for compact discs or cassette tapes.

INSTRUCTIONS

Construction involves making a closed box with top and bottom panels set in recesses along the inside edges of the sides. The lid is, in this sense, already part of the assembled box; it is simply cut from the box. The inner partition assembly is independent, and can be varied according to the use you plan for the case. It is fastened with a few screws to the inside of the box, and it can be removed easily.

Basic Cutting for the Box

Rip boards to 5⅛" width, then plane to ½" thickness. Before cutting the boards to length, use a router with a rabbet bit and cut a ¼" by ¼" rabbet along what will be the inside of the

SUPPLIES

- Twenty-four 1" No. 8 sheetrock screws
- Forty-eight ¾" wire brads
- Table saw and/or radial-arm saw
- Dado blades
- Drill, with 3/16" bit and ⅜" boring bit
- ⅜" plug cutter
- Walnut colored putty
- Phillips screwdriver
- Finishing sander
- Garnet paper, 60, 80, 120, and 180 grits
- Latches and handle hardware, as desired

MAKE TWO

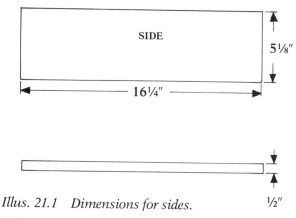

Illus. 21.1   Dimensions for sides.

MAKE TWO

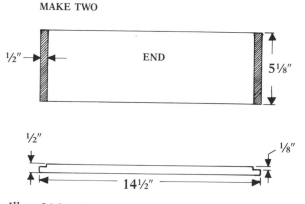

Illus. 21.2   Dimensions for ends, showing rabbets for lap joints.

82

Materials			Quantity
Walnut:	Box side	½″ × 5⅛″ × 16¼″	2
	Box end	½″ × 5⅛″ × 14½″	2
	Partition end	½″ × 2⅜″ × 13½″	2
	Partition (to fit)	½″ × 2⅜″ × 15″	3
Plywood:	Panel (to fit)	¼″ × 16⅜″ × 14⅛″	2

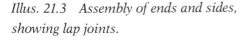

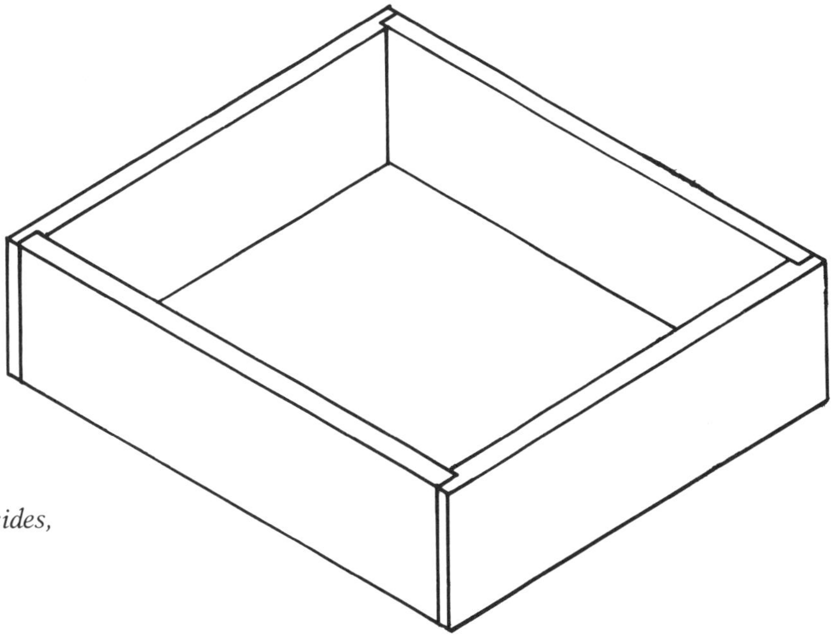

Illus. 21.3   Assembly of ends and sides, showing lap joints.

boards for both the top and bottom edges. These rabbets will allow the top and bottom panels to be recessed and fit flush with the sides.

Cut the sides (Illus. 21.1) and the ends (Illus. 21.2) to length. Cut a rabbet ⅛″ deep and ½″ wide along the inside edges for the front and back ends. These rabbets will allow the side pieces to be assembled with lap joints (Illus. 21.3). Counterbore halfway through the rabbets on the front and back ends with a ⅜″ boring bit, then drill a 3/16″ pilot hole through the remaining thickness (Illus. 21.4). Sand all parts with medium-grit garnet paper followed with fine grit. Assemble the sides and ends with glue and screws. Glue wood plugs in the counterbored holes to cover screwheads. After the glue dries, sand the plugs flush with the rest of the surface. Sand the top and bottom edges flush.

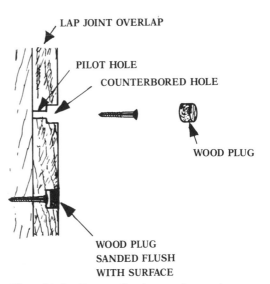

LAP JOINT OVERLAP

PILOT HOLE

COUNTERBORED HOLE

WOOD PLUG

WOOD PLUG
SANDED FLUSH
WITH SURFACE

Illus. 21.4   Counterboring and covering screwhead with wood plug.

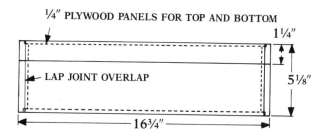

¼" PLYWOOD PANELS FOR TOP AND BOTTOM

1¼"

LAP JOINT OVERLAP

5⅛"

16¾"

Illus. 21.5   Box assembly showing thickness of lid and recessed placement of top and bottom panels. Side piece is shown overlapped by rabbets in end pieces.

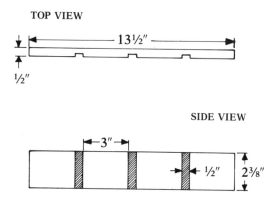

TOP VIEW

13½"

½"

SIDE VIEW

3"

½"   2⅜"

Illus. 21.6   Dimensions for ends of partition assembly showing dadoes for partitions.

Top and Bottom Panel Assembly

Cut the ¼" plywood to fit inside the recessed area. Attach the plywood top and bottom with glue and ¾" wire brads. Countersink the wire brads with a nail set. Sand all parts flush with medium grit garnet paper followed with fine grit.

Cutting the Lid from the Box

Set the table saw fence away from the blade the same distance as the thickness of the lid (Illus. 21.5). Mark at least one of the sides with a pencil line across the width to allow the lid to be replaced properly once it is sawed off. Set the height of the saw blade at ½". Rip around all four sides to separate the lid from the box.

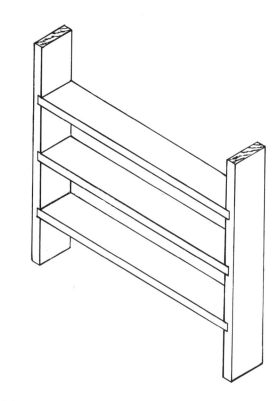

Illus. 21.7   Partition assembly.

Spacers the same thickness as the saw blade kerf should be used to hold the parts in place as the last side is ripped.

Inner Partition Assembly

Cut the two partition end parts to length, then make dado cuts as shown (Illus. 21.6). Counterbore and drill pilot holes for screws. Cut the three partitions to fit. Sand all parts with medium and fine grit garnet paper. Assemble the ends and partitions with screws (Illus. 21.7). Fit the partition assembly inside the box and secure with two screws at each end.

Finishing

Spray semi-gloss polyurethane finish over all surfaces as specified by the manufacturer. Attach the handle on one of the side pieces, and add latches, as desired, at either end to secure the lid to the case.

22 ♦ DEN OR FAMILY ROOM CLOCK

An uncomplicated and handsome project, this clock is rewarding to make for a favorite room in your home. It uses very little material, an oak base and walnut plugs, and so lends itself perfectly for gift making, allowing several to be constructed at the same time. The dark and light woods provide a pleasing contrast and an interesting complementary design in the circular face and the elliptical clock body.

SUPPLIES

- Band saw
- Router, with bits, template, and template guide
- ½" rounding-over router bit
- Drill, with bit and plug cutters
- Wood glue
- Garnet paper, 60, 80, 100, 120, and 220 grits
- Finish, as desired

MATERIALS

- Oak board, 1" × 8½" × 10"
- Scrap walnut board
- Clock movement

INSTRUCTION

The oak base is a full inch thick. Wood plugs are cut from scrap walnut to represent the numerals of the clock face. The plugs for the twelve o'clock, three o'clock, six o'clock, and nine o'clock positions are larger than the intervening positions.

Basic Cutting

Transfer the pattern for the clock to the oak board (Illus. 22.1). Follow the pattern and cut the oak board to the oval shape (Illus. 22.2). Rout the back of the oak board to accommodate the clock movement. Use a routing template of an appropriate dimension and a template guide on the router. Rout a step at a time until the proper depth is reached.

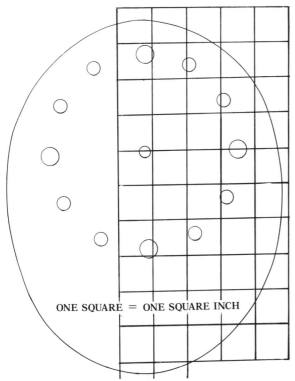

ONE SQUARE = ONE SQUARE INCH

Illus. 22.1   Pattern for clock face and body.

Illus. 22.2 Sawing out clock body on the band saw.

Illus. 22.3 Boring holes for the clock face "numerals."

Illus. 22.4 Cutting wood plugs for the clock face "numerals" out of walnut.

Preparing the Clock Face

Bore holes for the small and large dots on the clock face (Illus. 22.3). The larger holes should be ½" diameter and ¼" deep. The smaller ones should be ⅜" diameter and ¼" deep.

Cut wood plugs from the walnut scrap using plug-cutter bits (Illus. 22.4).

Glue the wood plugs in place with wood glue (Illus. 22.5). Each plug should extend out of its hole at least ⅛" to allow each to be sanded flush with the clock face surface. Allow the glue to dry thoroughly, then sand the plugs down flush with the clock surface.

Drill a hole for the stem of the clock movement. The stem will stick through from the back to allow the hands to be mounted in front.

Sand the edges of the oval shape to smooth any irregularities and remove saw marks. Rout around both the front and back edges of the clock body using a ½" rounding-over router bit.

Finishing

Sand all surfaces with garnet paper, proceeding from 60 to 80, 100, and 120 grits. Apply finish, as desired, sanding in between coats with 220 grit garnet paper.

Adding the Clock Movement

Assemble the clock movement, placing the stem through the hole and attaching the hands according to the manufacturer's directions.

Illus. 22.5 Gluing the walnut plugs in the holes for the clock face.

23 ◆ CRIBBAGE BOARD

The rich black walnut of this piece as pictured naturally brings a touch of elegance to any room. But you may already have a special piece of cherry or mahogany, which you feel would be just right for this piece; use what you prefer. The lid serves as the game board, when open. Small blocks at either end store the pegs and help keep a record of games won. Everything needed for the game stores within the case when the lid is closed.

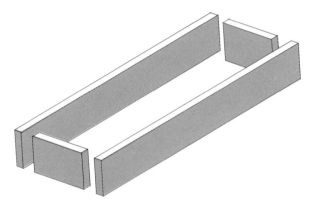

Illus. 23.1   Box construction.

INSTRUCTIONS

The construction of the cribbage board case is a simple box, with end pieces enclosed between two sides (Illus. 23.1). A bottom piece fits inside the end and side pieces, while the top piece fully covers the sides and ends flush with the outside surfaces (Illus. 23.2). The peg holders fit snug up against either end.

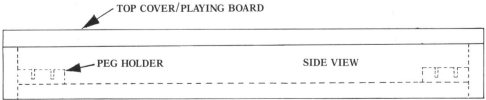

Illus. 23.2   Cribbage board case construction, layout of parts.

Materials			Quantity
Black walnut:	Ends	$3/8'' \times 1\,3/8'' \times 2\,3/4''$	2
	Sides	$3/8'' \times 1\,3/8'' \times 13''$	2
	Peg holders	$3/8'' \times 1'' \times 2\,3/4''$	2
	Bottom	$3/8'' \times 2\,3/4'' \times 12\,1/4''$	1
	Top	$3/8'' \times 3\,1/2'' \times 13''$	1
Dowel rod:	Pegs	$1/8''$ diameter $\times$ $5/8''$	16
Hardware:			
Small brass hinges			
Small brass latch			

SUPPLIES

- Saw
- Drill
- Wood glue
- Clamps
- Garnet paper, 60, 80, 100, 120, and 220 grits
- Red and black soft-tipped marking pens or paint, as desired
- Polyurethane varnish

Basic Cutting

From $3/8''$ thick walnut stock, cut pieces for the ends, sides, peg holders and bottom (Illus. 23.3). Sand all surfaces that will face inside after assembly. Sand progressively finer from 60 to 80, 100, and 120 grit paper.

From $1/8''$ diameter dowel rod, cut pegs $5/8''$ long. Taper the pegs slightly by careful sanding, and then color half of them black and half red by using soft-tipped marking pens or paint, as desired.

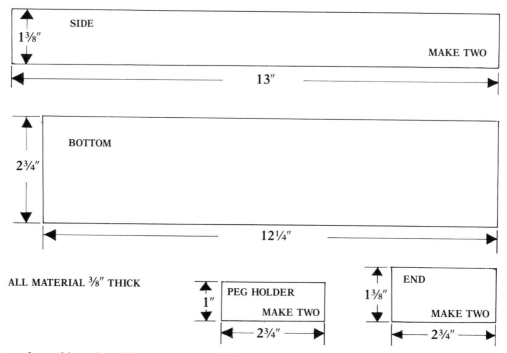

Illus. 23.3 Dimensions for cribbage board box pieces, excluding cover.

88

From the ⅜″ thick walnut stock, roughly cut a piece for the lid to serve as cover and playing board (Illus. 23.4). This piece will be fitted more precisely after the box is assembled. Fine-sand the underside playing board. Drill holes in the underside of the lid as indicated. Drill each hole to a ¼″ depth. The holes should be just slightly larger than the pegs, allowing for the taper. Drill the same size holes in the pieces that were cut for the peg holders. Space these holes as indicated (Illus. 23.2).

Assembly

Glue the sides to the ends, clamping until the glue is dry. Fit the bottom and glue in place, working the piece in from the bottom side of the box. Prepare a flat surface so that glue will not adhere to it, and then set the box flat on the surface, pressing the bottom and the sides down to ensure a flush fit. Install the peg holders with glue after the box assembly has dried.

Fit the top piece to the box assembly, and attach with hinges. Sand all outside surfaces flush. Progressively fine-sand the case, using each grit in turn.

Finishing

Apply polyurethane varnish according to the manufacturer's directions. Fine-sand with 220 grit paper after each coat has dried, but not sanding after the final coat.

Attach the latch and your cribbage board case is ready for play.

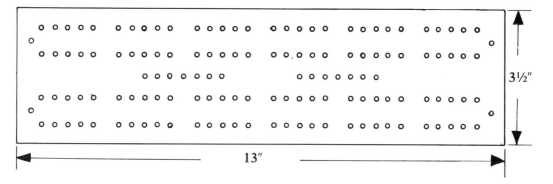

Illus. 23.4   Dimensions and layout for top cover/playing board.

This walnut curio cabinet will add beauty and a sumptuous aura to your collectibles as well as keep them dustfree and in pristine condition. The cabinet can be hung vertically or horizontally, and the partitions could be varied to suit the items you wish to display.

SUPPLIES

- Eight 1¼" No. 8 screws
- 1" wire brads
- Carpenter's glue
- Saw, with dado blade
- Router, with ¼" ogee bit, ⅜" Roman ogee bit
- Drill, with ⅜" counterboring bit, ⅛" bit
- Clamps
- Eight ⅜"-diameter 2" dowel pins
- Semi-gloss polyurethane spray finish

INSTRUCTIONS

The construction is essentially a simple box with lap joints to form the case, which has a frame lid with a clear pane. The inner parti-

Materials				Quantity
Walnut:	Case	side	¹³⁄₁₆″ × 3″ × 22⁹⁄₁₆″	2
		end	¹³⁄₁₆″ × 3″ × 19⅜″	2
	Lid	side	¹³⁄₁₆″ × 1¼″ × 23⅜″	2
		end	¹³⁄₁₆″ × 1¼″ × 17⅞″	2
	Partition assembly	side	½″ × 2⅜″ × 21⅝″	2
		cross-member	½″ × 2⅜″ × 17⅛″	4
		middle partition	½″ × 2⅜″ × 7⅜″	1
		side partition	½″ × 2⅜″ × 6½″	2
	Subdivisions	as needed	½″ × 2⅜″ × Cut to fit	
Walnut plywood:		bottom (to fit)	¼″ × 23″ × 18½″	1
Hardware:		Piano hinge (approx. 22″ long) Brass latch		
Plexiglas or single-strength glass (to fit)			⅛″ × 18½″ × 23″	1

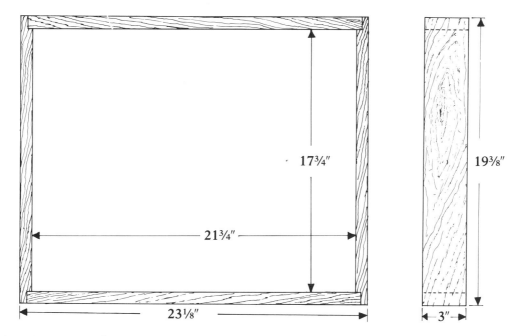

Illus. 24.1   Dimensions of case.

tion assembly is removable, and its design can be modified as desired. These three elements—the case, the frame lid, and the partition insert—are separately constructed and then assembled.

Basic Cutting for the Case

Rip materials for the sides and ends (Illus. 24.1), allowing ⅛″ for smoothing the edges on the jointer. Cut rabbets on each of the two end pieces for making lap joints. Sand all surfaces, progressing from 80 grit garnet paper to 120 and 180 grits.

Illus. 24.2   Assembly of end-to-side of case with screws.

Assembling the Case

Counterbore holes ⅜″ by ⅜″ at each screw location. Drill a ⅛″ pilot hole through the remaining thickness of the boards. Fasten ends to sides with screws (Illus. 24.2). Cover the screwheads by gluing ⅜″ diameter wood plugs in the counterbored holes. After the glue dries, sand the plugs flush with the surrounding surfaces.

Sand all joints flush, then rout around the inside bottom edges with a rabbeting bit to create a recess that will accommodate the ¼″ walnut plywood bottom. Cut the bottom plywood piece to fit, and secure with 1″ wire brads.

Frame Lid Assembly

Rip materials to width and smooth edges on the jointer. Cut parts to length as specified (Illus. 24.3). Glue and dowel the butt joints. After the glue dries, sand all joints flush. Rout a ¼″ by ¼″ rabbet on inside of the frame back to accommodate glass or Plexiglas. Rout the inside top edges of the frame with a ¼″ ogee bit. Rout around the outside top edges of the frame with a ⅜″ Roman ogee bit. Fine-sand all surfaces.

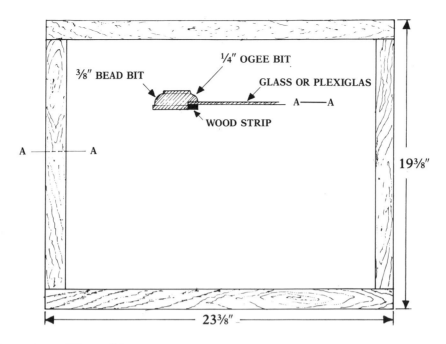

Illus. 24.3   Dimensions of frame lid.

Rout out for a piano hinge along the top edge of the case with a ½″ mortising bit. Attach the hinge to the case with screws, then to the lid. Secure the latch with screws.

Install ⅛″ Plexiglas or single-strength glass in the back side of the lid with either glazier's points or wood strips to hold it securely in place.

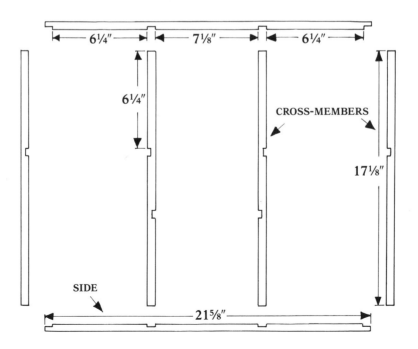

Partition Insert Assembly

Plane materials to ½" thickness, then rip to 2⅜" width. Cut piece for the two sides and four cross-members to length (Illus. 24.4). Lay out and cut the dadoes on each piece, and cut the rabbets on the ends of the side pieces. Assemble the sides and the cross-members using glue, wire brads, and screws. Keep the assembly square and secure with furniture clamps as needed.

Cut the partition pieces to fit in the dadoed slots. Glue these three pieces in place in the cross-member assembly. After glue dries, sand all joints flush. This assembly is the basic partition assembly (Illus. 24.5). At this point you can design your own subdivisions or use the plan of the finished cabinet pictured as a model (Illus. 24.6). Cut further subdividing partition pieces according to your plan, and glue in place. Sand all joints flush.

Finishing

It may be easier and more satisfying to finish the case and lid before the removable partition assembly is installed. The partition assembly can be finished at the same time so that when the last coat of polyurethane varnish is dry, the

Illus. 24.5   Basic partition assembly ready to be secured in case.

completed project can be simply assembled, ready to be hung.

A semi-gloss polyurethane finish is recommended; a spray is easy to apply. Allow each additional coat to dry thoroughly before a new coat is applied. Follow the manufacturer's directions, being sure to smooth between coats with 000 steel wool.

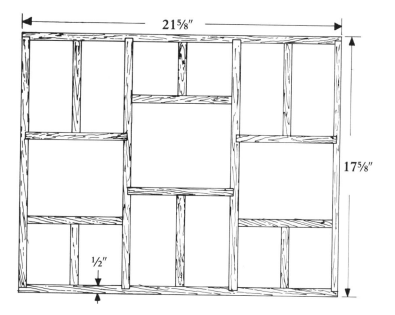

Illus. 24.6   Layout of one arrangement of subdivided partition assembly.

25 ◆ QUILT RACK

Display a treasured quilt or hand-crocheted Afghan on this striking quilt rack. The design accentuates the lap joints in the end feet support members by allowing the pieces to stand above the joining member ½″. This raised assembly produces a decorative effect that emphasizes the natural beauty of the wood.

Materials		Quantity
Top cross-member	1⅛″ × 4½″ × 20¼″	2
Feet	1⅛″ × 4½″ × 20¼″	2
Leg	1⅛″ × 5½″ × 30½″	2
Center support	1″ × 3½″ × 33½″	1
Bottom support	1″ × 1½″ × 33½″	2
Quilt hanger	1″ × 1½″ × 33½″	2
Handle (as desired)	¾″ × 5½″ × 33″	1

SUPPLIES

- Twenty 1¾″ No. 9 wood screws
- Eight 1¼″ No. 9 wood screws
- Plane
- Band saw
- Table saw or radial-arm saw, with dado blade or back saw with a wood chisel
- Router
- Drill, with ⅜″ and ³⁄₁₆″ bits
- Glue
- Wood plugs
- Garnet paper, 50, 80, 120, 180 grits
- 0000 steel wool
- Clear satin polyurethane finish

INSTRUCTIONS

The construction consists of supports joining two end assemblies. The end assemblies include feet, a vertical leg, and a top cross-member piece (Illus. 25.1). Connecting the top of the end assemblies are the quilt hangers on the outside and the handle in the middle.

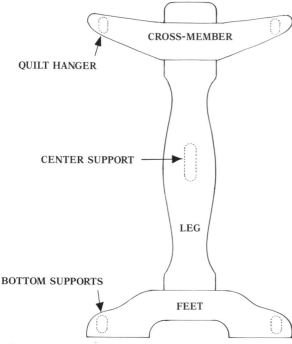

Illus. 25.1   End assembly, showing the location of connecting support pieces and quilt hangers.

POSITION OF LAP JOINT INDICATED BY DOTTED LINES.

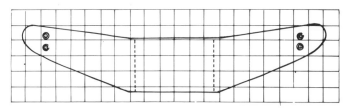

MAKE 2   FOR FULL-SIZE PATTERN, ENLARGE ON A 1″ GRID.

Illus. 25.2   Pattern for top cross-member, showing counterbored hole locations for screws to fasten quilt hangers.

POSITION OF LAP JOINT INDICATED BY DOTTED LINES.

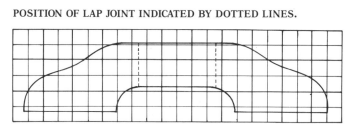

MAKE 2   FOR FULL-SIZE PATTERN, ENLARGE ON A 1″ GRID.

Illus. 25.3   Pattern for feet.

Basic Cutting

Enlarge patterns to full size for the top cross-members (Illus. 25.2), the feet (Illus. 25.3), and the legs (Illus. 25.4). Plane wood to the specified thickness of 1⅛″, then transfer the patterns to the wood. Using a band saw, cut the parts to shape.

On the table saw, rip one-inch thick boards to form the center support, lower supports, and quilt hangers (Illus. 25.5). When cutting to length, leave about 1″ extra on each board.

Also cut a ¾″ thick board to a slightly longer length than the 33″ specified for the handle. Lay out a design for the cutout and top of the handle, as desired. Cut the handle to shape.

Preparation for Assembly

Sand the surfaces of all of the parts, progressing from 50 grit to 80, 120, and 180. Rout a ¼″ radius on all corner edges except the ends that will butt against another piece.

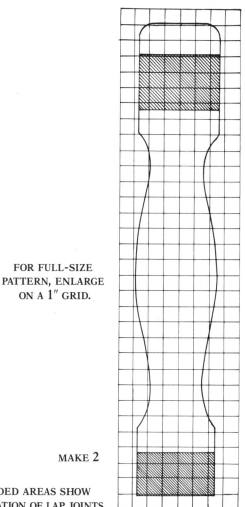

FOR FULL-SIZE
PATTERN, ENLARGE
ON A 1″ GRID.

MAKE 2

SHADED AREAS SHOW
LOCATION OF LAP JOINTS.

Illus. 25.4   Pattern for legs.

CENTER SUPPORT

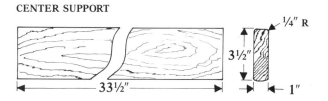

QUILT HANGERS AND BOTTOM SUPPORTS

MAKE 4

Illus. 25.5   Dimensions for the center supports, and for the quilt hangers and bottom supports.

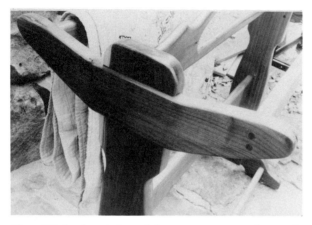

Illus. 25.6   Lap joint of the top cross-member and the leg, showing the ½" relief between the joined parts and the continuous rounding on the outside edge of the top cross-member piece.

Counterbore holes ⅜" in diameter by ⅜" deep at each screw location. Drill a ³⁄₁₆" pilot hole through the remaining thickness of the boards.

Cut the gains (notches) for joining the top cross-members and feet to the legs. The gains are cut only ⅜" deep rather than halfway through each board. The joined pieces will stick out ½" (Illus. 25.6). Joining in this manner allows the pieces to be routed with a radius before assembly. A dado blade on a table saw or radial-arm saw is the easiest method to cut the gains. Hand tools such as a back saw and wood chisel would work equally well.

Assembly

Lay out the parts and fit them together to check each joint for accuracy. When you are satisfied with a proper fit, use screws to join the parts. Fasten the two bottom supports, two quilt hangers, handle, and center support to the assembled ends. Glue wood plugs in the counterbored holes to cover the screwheads. Each plug should stand above the surface. After the glue is dry, sand the plugs flush.

Finishing

After assembly and the wood plugs have been sanded flush, check all areas for smoothness. Sand where needed. Use a clear satin polyurethane finish, following the manufacturer's directions. Apply at least three coats, allowing each coat to dry before applying the next. Smooth with 0000 steel wool between coats.

26 ◆ GUN RACK

This attractive oak gun rack offers a functional way to put one or two prized guns on display. A storage space with sliding doors accommodates cleaning equipment, ammunition, and other small items.

SUPPLIES

- Screws
- Wood glue
- Table saw or radial-arm saw
- Router, with ¼″ rounding-over bit
- Drill
- Wood plugs
- Garnet paper, 80, 100, 150, and 220 grit
- Stain and finish, as desired

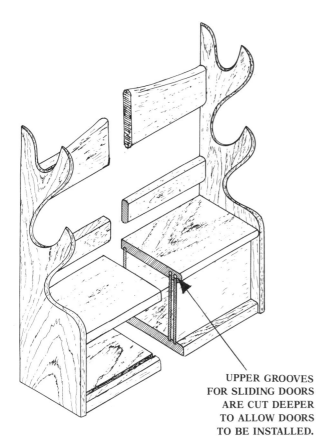

UPPER GROOVES
FOR SLIDING DOORS
ARE CUT DEEPER
TO ALLOW DOORS
TO BE INSTALLED.

Illus. 26.1   Cutaway view of gun rack.

Materials		Quantity
End	¾″ × 7½″ × 29½″	2
Top rail	¾″ × 6″ × 23″	1
Lower rail	¾″ × 1½″ × 23″	1
Top of compartment	¾″ × 7⅛″ × 23″	1
Bottom of compartment	¾″ × 7⅛″ × 23″	1
Plywood door	¼″ × 7½″ × 11⅝″	2
Plywood back	¼″ × 7½″ × 23″	1

INSTRUCTIONS

Construction is straightforward if you follow through the directions closely, but a few elements need to be noted. Two end pieces are butt-jointed to the back rails and top and bottom of the storage compartment. The sliding doors fit in grooves, but in order to be installed the upper groove must be deeper (Illus. 26.1).

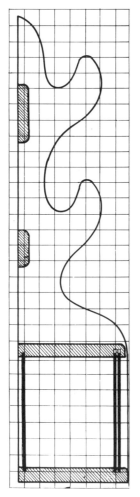

Illus. 26.2   Pattern for ends of gun rack, showing locations of butt joints to other pieces.

Basic Cutting

Enlarge the patterns for the ends (Illus. 26.2) and the top rail (Illus. 26.3). Transfer the patterns to the wood and cut the pieces to shape.

Cut pieces to the proper dimensions for the lower rail (Illus. 26.4) and the top (Illus. 26.5) and the bottom (Illus. 26.6) of the storage compartment.

Make the doors and back (to fit) from ¼″ plywood, cutting to shape (Illus. 26.7).

Preparation for Assembly

Sand all surfaces, progressing from 80 to 100 and 150 grit. Rout the edges of the pieces as indicated in the drawings. Fine-sand all of the parts with 220-grit garnet paper.

Counterbore ⅜″-diameter holes ⅜″ deep for the screwheads, and drill pilot holes for the screw shank.

Assembly

Using glue and screws, assemble the parts. Cover the screws with wood plugs cut from the same wood used in the project (Illus. 26.8). After the glue has dried, sand the wood plugs flush.

Finishing

Apply stain, as desired, and allow to dry. Apply a protective finish, as desired, following the manufacturer's directions.

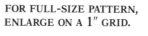
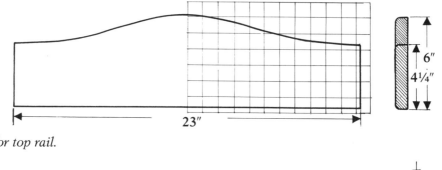

Illus. 26.3   Pattern for top rail.

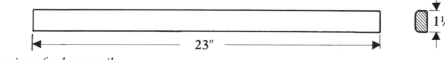

Illus. 26.4   Dimensions for lower rail.

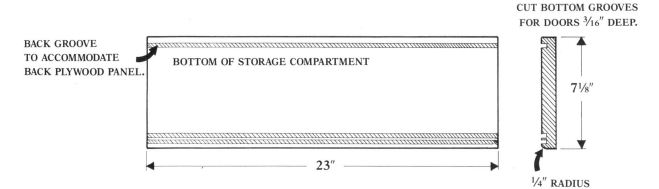

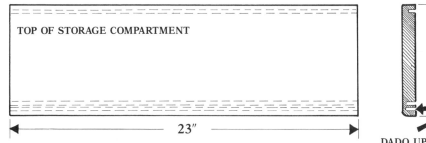

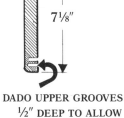

TOP OF STORAGE COMPARTMENT

23"

7⅛"

DADO UPPER GROOVES
½" DEEP TO ALLOW
DOORS TO BE INSTALLED.

Illus. 26.5   Dimensions for top of storage compartment, showing location and depth of the grooves for the sliding doors and the back.

CUT BOTTOM GROOVES
FOR DOORS ³⁄₁₆" DEEP.

BACK GROOVE
TO ACCOMMODATE
BACK PLYWOOD PANEL.

BOTTOM OF STORAGE COMPARTMENT

23"

7⅛"

¼" RADIUS

Illus. 26.6   Dimensions for the bottom of storage compartment, showing location and depth of the grooves for the sliding door and the back.

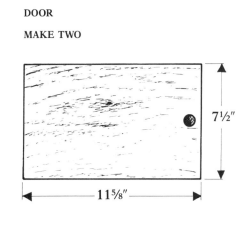

DOOR

MAKE TWO

7½"

11⅝"

USE ¼" PLYWOOD

Illus. 26.7   Dimensions for sliding doors.

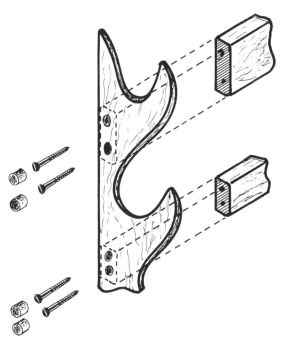

Illus. 26.8   End and rail assembly, showing butt joints to be fastened with screws, which are then covered with plugs.

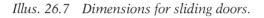

27 ◆ MARBLEIZED SHELF

Materials		Quantity
White pine	$1'' \times 12'' \times 48''$	one board

SUPPLIES
(for woodworking)

- Eighteen 1½" No. 8 hardboard screws
- Eighteen ⅜" × ½" wood plugs
- Saw
- Router, with ⅜" rounding-over bit
- Drill, with ⅜" boring bit
- Garnet paper, 60, 80, 100, 120, and 180 grit

SUPPLIES
(for marbleizing)

- One flat bristle cutter brush
- Two 2" polyfoam brushes
- Brown paper bag
- Newspaper
- Practice paper or prepared wood
- Plastic wrap
- Medium-size sea wool sponge
- Paper towels
- Sharp-cornered art eraser
- Turkey feather
- Acrylic paint for basecoat
- Clear and colored glaze
- Mineral spirits

Even if you haven't done any decorative paint-work before, you can enjoy making this mar-bleized shelf, and be pleased with your results. When you are ready to marbleize the shelf, you will have the opportunity to practice the techniques you will need until you feel ready to start.

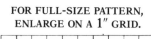

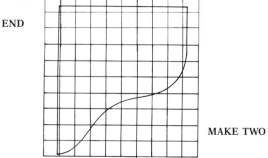

Illus. 27.1   Pattern for the ends.

INSTRUCTIONS

The shelf construction is uncomplicated. Two ends support the main top shelf, while the lower shelf is butt-jointed to the ends. Both shelves have a support piece running along the back.

Basic Cutting

Enlarge the pattern to full size for the ends (Illus. 27.1). Transfer the pattern to wood and cut out both pieces. Following the dimensions, cut pieces for the top shelf (Illus. 27.2), the lower shelf (Illus. 27.3), and the shelf supports (Illus. 27.4).

Preparation for Assembly

Sand all surfaces with 60-grit garnet paper, followed by 80 grit. Rout the edges and ends of the top shelf using a ⅜" rounding-over bit. Rout the front edges of the lower shelf and the ends.

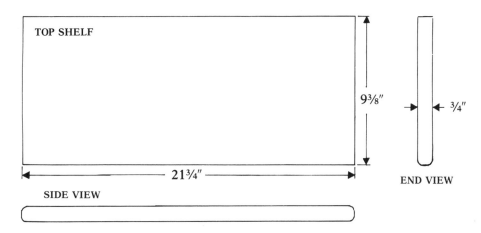

Illus. 27.2   Dimensions for the top shelf.

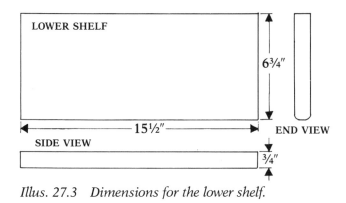

Illus. 27.3   Dimensions for the lower shelf.

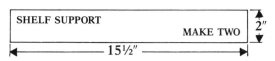

Illus. 27.4   Dimensions for the shelf supports.

Illus. 27.5   Counterbored hole so that screwhead can be covered with a wood plug.

Sand all of the parts with 100-grit paper, followed by 120 grit. Counterbore holes for screwheads in the ends and top shelf, ⅜″ in diameter and about halfway through the thickness. Drill pilot holes for the screw shanks through the remaining thickness (Illus. 27.5).

Assembly

Using screws, assemble the shelf supports and lower shelf between the ends. Glue plugs in the counterbored holes to cover the screwheads. After the glue dries, sand the plugs flush with the surface of the end boards.

After all of the surfaces are fine-sanded, secure the top shelf with screws. Glue plugs in the counterbored holes, and sand flush after the glue dries. Fine-sand the top shelf and other parts where needed with 180-grit garnet paper.

Marbleizing by Susan Stallman

Prepare the unfinished wood shelf by sanding until smooth and then wiping clean. Apply a basecoat of acrylic paint of the appropriate color, using a polyfoam brush. When dry, buff the surface with a piece of brown paper bag until smooth. Apply a second coat, let dry, and buff again.

The four techniques you will be using are brushed-on glaze, nonveined marble, negative veins, and positive veins. Cover your work table with newspaper and practice each of these techniques on practice paper or on a piece of wood prepared just as the shelf has been.

Brushing on Glaze

When you have practiced and are ready to start, place the shelf upside down on the work surface. Working carefully on one support at a time, brush on a liberal application of glaze. Loosely crumple a 12″ piece of plastic wrap, and press it onto the wet glaze and lift. If you mess up, brush on more glaze and try again. Complete the mottling of one support and move on to the next.

Sponging Nonveined Marble

You may mottle the entire shelf or, if in doubt, work in sections. Again, apply glaze liberally and mottle as described above. To create non-veined marble, dampen a sponge with mineral spirits, and press onto the wet mottling, fashioning soft drifts which flow across at about a 45 degree angle. Immediately crumple paper towel, and press over the sponged areas to remove even more glaze and create drifts.

Using an Eraser for Negative Veins

Form negative veins by pressing the corners of an eraser into the glaze and pulling in a nervous, jerky motion to expose the background. If necessary, cut the eraser in half with a knife for good sharp corners. Twist and turn the eraser as you pull, and wipe often with a rag or paper towel. Veins can be softened by patting lightly with the tip of a bristle brush. You may wish to stop at this point or go on.

Painting on Positive Veins

Positive veins should flow in the same general direction as the drifts. Dip a turkey feather into a mixture of colored and clear glazes and paint on veins. Soften by brushing lightly with a bristle brush.

Sealing

Wait twenty-four to forty-eight hours for the glaze to completely dry. Then apply varnish, following the manufacturer's directions.

Country Kitchen Accents

28 ◆ MUG RACK

This sturdy mug rack made of oak will add a touch of country style to your kitchen. The rack accommodates eight mugs and provides a convenient place to keep the sugar bowl and cream pitcher. This project makes a great housewarming gift that will also showcase your woodworking.

SUPPLIES

- Band saw
- Router, with Roman ogee bit, and ⅜″ rounding-over bit
- Lathe
- Mallet
- Oil or bee's wax
- Drill, with drill press table
- Garnet paper, 50, 80, 100, 150, 220 grits
- 0000 steel wool
- Polyurethane finish

INSTRUCTIONS

Several design alternatives might be applied in making this mug holder. Six cups might be ample rather than eight. A round base might be more pleasing than oval. The column size might also be changed. In making the holder described here it will be assumed that a lathe is available and an eight mug capacity is needed.

Basic Cutting

Enlarge the pattern for the base to full-size (Illus. 28.1). Using a band saw or other tool capable of making curved cuts, saw the base to shape. Sand all surfaces, first with coarse grit garnet paper (50–80), followed with medium grit (100–150).

Materials		Quantity
Base	1½″ × 11″ × 13″	1
Column	2″ × 2″ × 18½″	1
Wood ball (If needed)	2″ diameter	1
Dowel for pegs	⅜″ × 3¼″	8
Dowel pin (for ball)	⅜″ × 2″	1

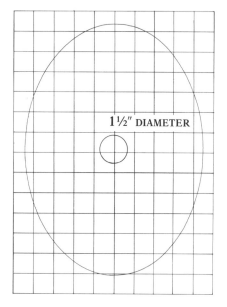

1½″ DIAMETER

Illus. 28.1   Pattern for base, showing location of ¾″ deep hole to accommodate round tenon on column.

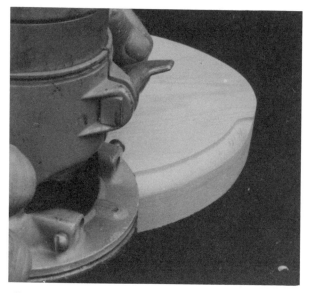

Illus. 28.2   Routing the top edge of the base with a Roman ogee bit.

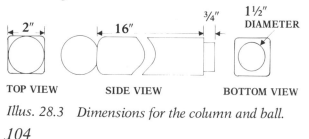

2″   16″   ¾″   1½″ DIAMETER

TOP VIEW   SIDE VIEW   BOTTOM VIEW

Illus. 28.3   Dimensions for the column and ball.

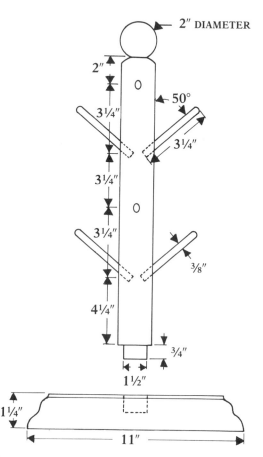

2″ DIAMETER

2″

50°

3¼″

3¼″

3¼″

3¼″

⅜″

4¼″

¾″

1½″

1¼″

11″

Illus. 28.4   Dimensions and locations for dowel pegs, round tenon, and ball on column.

Rout around the top edge with a Roman ogee bit (Illus. 28.2). Bore a 1½″-diameter hole ¾″ deep in the middle for mounting the column to the base. Fine-sand all surfaces with fine grit garnet paper (180–220).

Cut the column board to dimensions, leaving 1″ on each end for chucking in the lathe (Illus. 28.3). Rout lengthwise down each corner of the column with a ⅜″ rounding-over bit. Mark locations of ⅜″ dowel holes along length of column (Illus. 28.4).

Tilt the drill press table at 40 degrees. Drill the holes ¾″ deep. To help prevent the drill from drifting as it starts, hold the column up horizontally to start the drill, then gradually lower it back to the tilted table to drill the remainder of the hole. Note: the column board must rest on the inclined drill press table so that it is aligned with the drill bit.

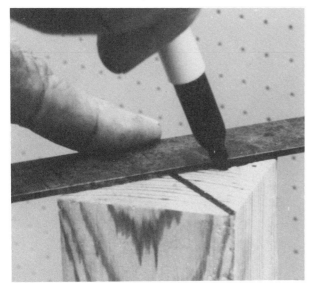

Illus. 28.5 Marking diagonal to locate placement of lathe center in piece for column.

Turning the Column

Draw diagonals from corner to corner across each end to locate center (Illus. 28.5). Saw a kerf along each diagonal line on the live center end of the board. Make a small hole in the center of each end with a small drill bit or sharpened nail.

Remove the spur and taper (live center) from the lathe headstock. Tap the spur and center with a mallet (Illus. 28.6). Place the spur back in the lathe headstock.

Remove the dead center from the tailstock and set it in the other end of the wood by tapping it with a mallet. Replace the dead center in the tailstock.

Chuck the column board between lathe centers, making sure tailstock and dead center are locked in place (Illus. 28.7). A drop or two of oil or a small piece of bee's wax placed between the dead center and the wood will help prevent heat caused by the friction of the wood turning on the metal center. Stop the lathe at frequent intervals and check to make sure the wood is secure between centers.

Set the lathe speed at medium or low for the first cut. Adjust the tool rest and lock it in place, then turn the wood by hand to assure clearance.

Illus. 28.6 Tapping the lathe center in place with a mallet.

Illus. 28.7 Checking the placement of the column between the lathe centers.

Turn the round tenon on the bottom of the column to fit the 1½″ hole cut previously in the base.

The ball on top of the column can either be turned on the lathe or purchased at a hardware supplier and secured to the top of the column with a dowel and glue.

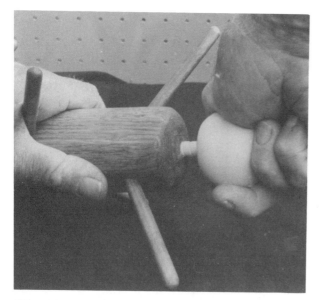

Illus. 28.8   Rather than turn the ball top of the column, a ball of the appropriate size can be purchased and attached to the column with glue and dowel.

Illus. 28.9   Preparing to assemble the column with pegs to the oval base by inserting the round tenon of the column in the hole prepared in the base.

Assembly

Fine-sand all surfaces of the column with fine grit garnet paper. Secure ⅜″ dowels in holes along column length.

If the ball on top is not turned, drill a hole at the top of the column and in the ball to fit a ⅜″ diameter dowel. Attach the ball to the top of the column, using a 2″-long dowel and glue (Illus. 28.8).

Assemble the column to the base with glue (Illus. 28.9).

Finishing

Apply polyurethane finish in three thin coats, allowing specified drying time between coats. Sand lightly between coats with 220-grit garnet paper or 0000 steel wool.

29 ◆ NAPKIN HOLDER

This napkin holder offers a simple, but elegant way to keep paper napkins handy in your kitchen or dining area. The assembly is straightforward, but the beauty of the finished piece—the smooth lines and fine grain—adds a touch of grace and richness to your table.

SUPPLIES

- Four 1½″ No. 8 flat-head wood screws
- Two 1¼″ No. 8 flat-head wood screws
- Saw
- Router, with a ⅜″ rounding-over bit
- Drill, with ⅜″ counterbore, ³⁄₁₆″ drill, and ⅛″ pilot hole bits
- Garnet paper, 60, 80, 100, and 120 grit
- Self-adhesive felt, one square foot
- Finish, as desired

Materials		Quantity
Base	¾″ × 7⅜″ × 10⅛″	1
Hold-down board	½″ × 2¾″ × 10⅛″	1
Upright	¾″ × 1¼″ × 3½″	2
Handle	¾″ × 1¼″ × 4″	1

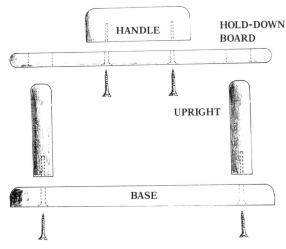

Illus. 29.1 Napkin holder assembly.

INSTRUCTIONS

The construction is made up of five parts, two of which are the same (Illus. 29.1). Assembly is accomplished without glue, fastening the project with six screws. The napkin holder pictured is made of wild cherry wood, but many other woods are suitable.

Basic Cutting

Lay out and cut wood pieces into starting rectangles for the base (Illus. 29.2), the hold-down board (Illus. 29.3), the handle and the two uprights (Illus. 29.4). Mark the round corners on both the base and the hold-down board. Cut the round corners on the band saw or other saw capable of cutting curves.

Preparation for Assembly

Sand all edges of the boards with 60-grit garnet paper. Lay out and drill the ⅞″-diameter holes on the hold-down board. Note how the holes overlap to produce the larger opening (Illus. 29.3). Draw a straight line connecting the outside edges of the overlapping holes, and cut the sides along the line to shape the oval opening.

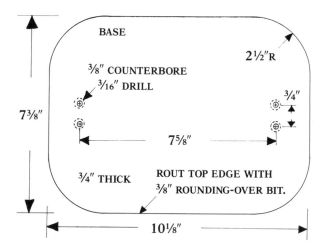

Illus. 29.2 Dimensions for base.

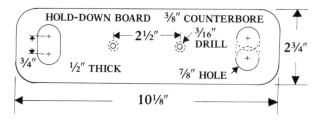

Illus. 29.3 Dimensions for hold-down board.

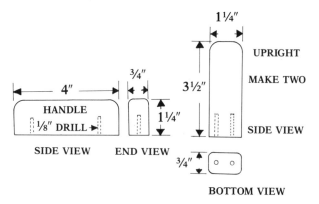

Illus. 29.4 Dimensions for handle and uprights.

Sand the inside edges of the oval holes by wrapping garnet paper around a rod, oval-shaped or round. Sand progressively with 60-grit garnet paper followed by 80, 100, and 120 grit. Rout or sand the edges of both the hold-down board and the base to produce the rounding-over look. Sand all flat surfaces progressively, starting with 60 grit, followed by 80, 100, and 120 grit garnet paper. Use a sanding block—any small wood block wrapped in garnet paper—to sand the flat surfaces, but sand the rounded edges by hand.

Drill ³⁄₁₆″ holes in the base and the hold-down board. Counterbore with a ³⁄₈″ bit on the underside of both pieces. Drill pilot holes in the handle and the upright by first drilling only one of the pair. Use a ¹⁄₈″ drill bit. Before drilling the second pilot hole, fasten the pieces together with one screw only.

Final Assembly

Examine the partial assembly—with the single screw holding each piece—and carefully align the uprights on the base. Check to see that the hold-down board moves smoothly up and down the uprights, and that the uprights fit loosely through the oval openings in the hold-down board. Make adjustments until you are satisfied. Then check the alignment once again for the uprights, and drill the second ¹⁄₈″ pilot hole for each pair of uprights.

Similarly, align the handle carefully on the hold-down board, then drill the remaining pilot hole. Drive the remaining screws.

Finishing

Apply finish, as desired, following the manufacturer's directions. After the last coat of finish is thoroughly dry, apply self-adhesive felt to the underside of the base. Trim any excess from around the edges.

30 ◆ TELEPHONE SHELF

The country look of this telephone shelf makes it just right for the kitchen, but it could as easily find a place in your family room—or even the front hall. This decorative addition is immensely practical. The phone is up and out of the way, a handy tray on the side holds notepads and pens or pencils, a writing desk pulls out easily, and there is a shelf to hold the local directory.

SUPPLIES

- Table saw
- Router, with ⅜″ rounding-over bit
- Drill, with ⅜″ counterbore and ⅛″ bit
- 1¼″ No. 8 screws
- Wood plugs, cut using ⅜″ plug cutter
- Finishing nails
- Nail set
- Colored putty
- Garnet paper, 50, 80, 100, 150, 180, and 220 grit
- Stain
- Polyurethane varnish
- ¾″ wood knob

INSTRUCTIONS

The telephone shelf pictured is made of inexpensive white pine, but many woods are suitable. Before you construct the design as given, you may want to look closely at the dimensions of your local telephone directory to make sure it will fit comfortably between the shelves. You may need to adjust the spacing slightly between shelves, and perhaps the height of the back piece and length of the sides to accommodate your local directory (Illus. 30.1).

Basic Cutting

Enlarge the patterns to full size for the sides (Illus. 30.2) and the top piece (Illus. 30.3). Cut the remaining pieces that are mounted between the sides—the back (Illus. 30.4), the shelves (Illus. 30.5), and the bottom (Illus. 30.6)—to the same width as the top piece.

Cut the pieces for the pull-out writing desk and desk front (Illus. 30.7) ⅛″ less wide than the other pieces, so that they will have sufficient clearance to slide in and out smoothly.

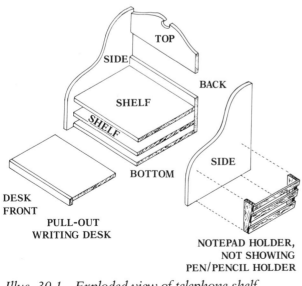

Illus. 30.1 Exploded view of telephone shelf.

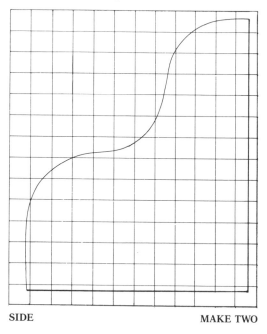

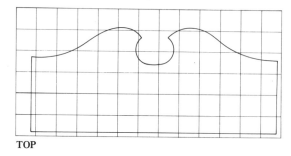

Illus. 30.3   Pattern for top piece.

Illus. 30.2   Pattern for sides.

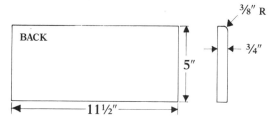

Illus. 30.4   Dimensions for back.

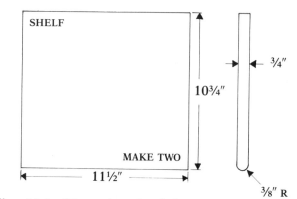

Illus. 30.5   Dimensions for shelves.

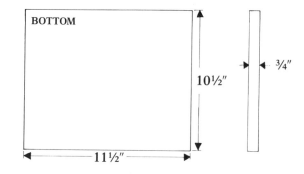

Illus. 30.6   Dimensions for bottom.

Materials		Quantity
Sides	³⁄₄″ × 12⁵⁄₈″ × 13″	2
Top	³⁄₄″ × 5″ × 11½″	1
Back	³⁄₄″ × 5″ × 11½″	1
Shelves	³⁄₄″ × 10³⁄₄″ × 11½″	2
Bottom	³⁄₄″ × 10½″ × 11½″	1
Pull-out writing desk	³⁄₄″ × 8½″ × 11³⁄₈″	1
Desk front	³⁄₄″ × 1¼″ × 11³⁄₈″	1
Notepad holder sides	½″ × 1½″ × 4⁵⁄₈″	2
Notepad holder slats	¼″ × 1″ × 8½″	3
Notepad holder bottom	½″ × ³⁄₄″ × 7½″	1
Pen/pencil holder	1¼″ × 1³⁄₈″ × 3³⁄₈″	1

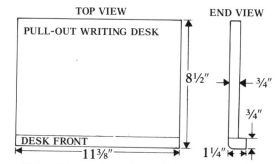

Illus. 30.7   Dimensions for pull-out writing desk and desk front.

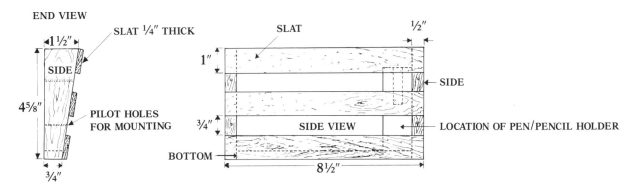

Illus. 30.8   Dimensions for notepad holder.

Cut the slats, sides, and bottom piece for the notepad holder (Illus. 30.8). Cut a solid wood piece for the pen/pencil holder (Illus. 30.9).

Preparation for Assembly
Sand all surfaces progressively with 50-grit garnet paper, followed by 80, 100, 150, 180, and 220 grit. Rout the edges as shown on the drawings, using a ⅜″ rounding-over bit. Mark screw locations, then counterbore a ⅜″-diameter hole halfway through the piece. Drill a ⅛″ pilot hole through the remaining thickness.

Assembly
Attach the two side pieces to the top piece (Illus. 30.10) using 1¼″ No. 8 screws. Install the upper shelf between the sides using two gauge blocks to hold the shelf in place while

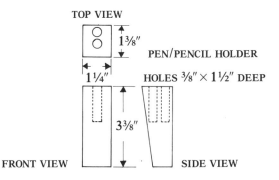

Illus. 30.9   Dimensions for pen/pencil holder.

the screws are driven. Using gauge blocks cut to the proper thickness, place the lower shelf between the sides. With the lower shelf held securely in place, drive the mounting screws. Install the bottom in the same manner.

Attach the desk front piece to the pull-out writing desk using glue and finishing nails.

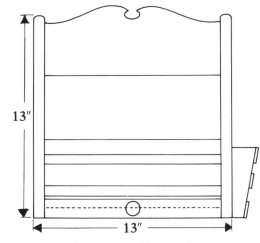

Illus. 30.10   Telephone shelf assembly.

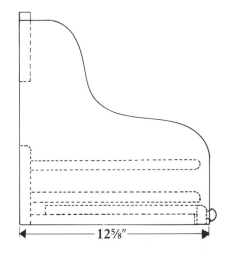

Set the heads of the finishing nails below the surface with a nail set. Attach a ¾" wood knob to the front of the writing desk assembly.

Assemble the notepad holder sides, slats and bottom (Illus. 30.8). Check the fit of the pen/pencil holder (Illus. 30.9) and make necessary adjustments. Attach the notepad holder assembly to the side of the shelf assembly using finishing nails, driven through the pilot holes. Insert and attach the pen/pencil holder.

Cover the screwheads with wood plugs, preferably cut from the same wood as the project. Each plug is glued in the counterbored hole and left sticking out so that it can be sanded flush after the glue dries.

Finishing

Check all surfaces and fine-sand where necessary. When you are satisfied with the smoothness, take care to remove all dust from the wood.

Apply stain, as desired, according to the manufacturer's directions. Allow the assembly to dry for at least six hours. Apply polyurethane varnish following the manufacturer's directions. Sand lightly between coats with 220-grit garnet paper or smooth with steel wool. Fill the small holes on the front of the pull-out writing desk—where the nail heads were set below the surface—with colored putty.

31 ◆ HARDWOOD STOOL

The construction of this handsome, dependable stool provides it with extra sturdiness. The type of wood you choose can also contribute further to the strength of the stool. The stool pictured was made of oak, but walnut, ash, or other hardwood will make a sturdy stool.

SUPPLIES

- Saw
- Router, with ⅜″ rounding-over bit
- Drill, with ⅜″ counterbore, ⅛″ bit
- Garnet paper, 50, 100, 120, 150, 220 grits
- Half-round wood file
- Six 1¼″ No. 9 flat-head wood screws
- Six 1″ No. 8 flat-head wood screws
- ⅜″ wood plugs, preferably the same wood as project
- Wood glue
- Stain or paint, as desired
- Polyurethane varnish, as desired

Illus. 31.1   Legs attached to the middle support assembly.

Materials		Quantity
Crosspiece	¾″ × 5″ × 11″	1
Support	¾″ × 2″ × 12″	1
Legs	¾″ × 7¾″ × 9″	2
Stool top	¾″ × 9″ × 17″	1

INSTRUCTIONS

Whether you use hardwood or a softwood, the construction method will ensure a strong and sturdy stool. The main feature of the design is that the legs join to a middle support assembly (Illus. 31.1). This support assembly also attaches directly to the stool top, effectively redistributing and supporting the load as someone steps on the top.

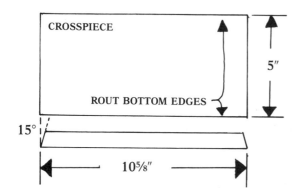

Illus. 31.2   Dimensions for crosspiece.

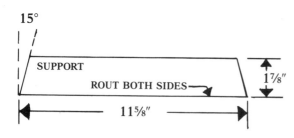

Illus. 31.3   Dimensions for support.

Basic Cutting

Cut the wood parts to shape for the crosspiece (Illus. 31.2), the support (Illus. 31.3), the legs (Illus. 31.4), and the stool top (Illus. 31.5). If you prefer, cut the crosspiece and support longer than needed so that the angle can be cut all at once later. Sand all of the parts with coarse or medium (50-100) grit garnet paper. Use a wood file (Illus. 31.6) to sand the inside curves on the legpieces, or use sandpaper wrapped around a cylindrical object.

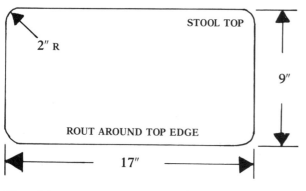

Illus. 31.5   Dimensions for stool top.

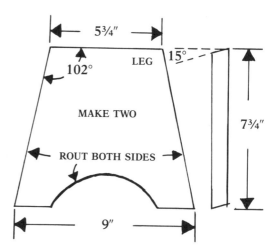

Illus. 31.4   Dimensions for legs.

Rout the edges of the parts as indicated, using a ⅜″ rounding-over bit. Locate screw holes and counterbore ⅜″-diameter holes for about half the thickness, drilling pilot holes for the screw shanks for the remaining thickness.

Assembly

Sand the crosspiece and the support with medium and then fine (150-220) grit garnet paper. Join the crosspiece to the support using 1¼″ screws (Illus. 31.7). If you cut the crosspiece and the support longer than required, the ends can be sawed cleanly to the proper angle once the pieces are fastened to each other.

Illus. 31.6   Shaping inside curves with half-round wood file.

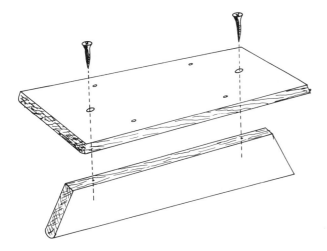

Illus. 31.7   Crosspiece joining to support with 1¼″ screws.

Fine-sand the inside surface of the legs, then assemble the legs to the middle support assembly (Illus. 31.1). The legs can be attached by attaching one leg completely with three screws, and then securing the second leg with only one screw. Find the correct screw locations in the middle support assembly by plac-ing the partially assembled stool on a flat surface. Make sure the legs are level, and mark the orientation. Drive the remaining screws.

Glue wood plugs in the counterbored holes in the legs. After the glue dries, but before attaching the stool top, sand the plugs flush. If additional sanding is necessary, sand progressively first with 100, then with 120, 150, and 220 grit.

Place the stool top on a clean, flat surface with the bottom side up. Arrange the leg and support assembly upside down on the stool top. Check for proper alignment, and join the assembly to the top using 1″ screws.

Finishing

Paint or apply stain following the manufacturer's directions.

Apply polyurethane finish, as desired, according to the manufacturer's directions. Allow each coat to dry thoroughly before applying a new coat. Sand between coats with 220-grit garnet paper, or smooth with steel wool.

This apothecary case adds character to your kitchen counter while providing a multitude of new storage nooks. Cases like this were once the mainstays of the late nineteenth–early twentieth century pharmacists who used them to store prescription medicines. The many drawers are just right for storing your spices, keeping kitchen wares handy, or putting collectibles safely out of harm's way.

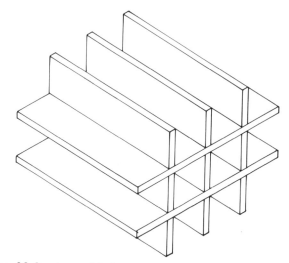

INSIDE PARTITIONS INTERLOCK TO FORM DRAWER COMPARTMENTS.

Illus. 32.2   Assembled partitions.

INSTRUCTIONS

The construction of the case begins with a partition assembly; sets of interlocking partitions are joined by sliding together (Illus. 32.1) without the need for mechanical fasteners.

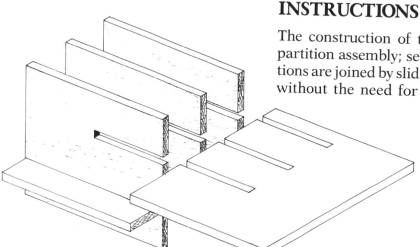

Illus. 32.1   Interlocking partition boards form the core of the apothecary case.

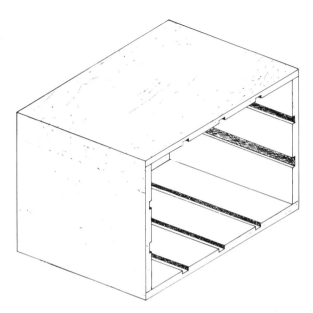

Illus. 32.3   Assembled case showing dadoes for partition assembly.

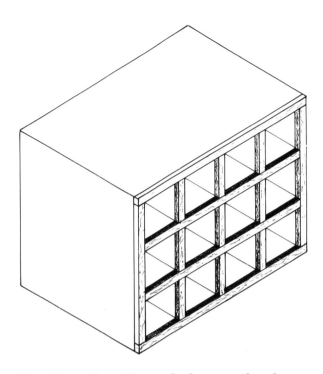

Illus. 32.4   The addition of a facing readies the case for the drawers.

The assembled partitions (Illus. 32.2) slide into the assembled ends and sides of the case along dadoes (Illus. 32.3). The front of the case—partitions and the outer edges—are covered with facing made from the same material as the case and drawer front (Illus. 32.4). The drawers are a simple box (Illus. 32.5) to which the drawer fronts are attached along with appropriate knobs.

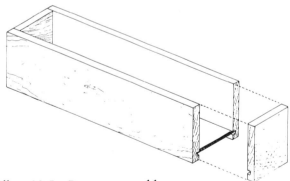

Illus. 32.5   Drawer assembly.

SUPPLIES

- 1″ panelling nails
- Thirty-six 1¼″ No. 8 sheetrock screws
- Wood plugs cut from same material as case
- 1″ No. 6 screws
- Table saw or radial-arm saw
- Dado blades
- Band saw
- Planer
- Router, with ¼″ rounding-over bit
- Drill, with ⅜″ boring bit, ⅛″ twist drill
- Wood glue
- Hammer
- Nail set
- Screwdriver
- Try square
- Steel tape
- Garnet paper, coarse, medium, and fine grits
- Satin polyurethane finish
- Twelve porcelain knobs, as desired

Materials			Quantity
Partitions (plywood)	horizontal	¾″ × 15¼″ × 18¾″	2
	vertical	¾″ × 15¼″ × 14″	3
Case (walnut)	sides	¾″ × 16″ × 19¾″	2
	ends	¾″ × 15″ × 16″	2
	back	¾″ × 19¼″ × 15½″	1
Drawer sides (white pine)		½″ × 3⅞″ × 15¼″	24
Drawer ends (white pine)		½″ × 2⅞″ × 3⅞″	24
Drawer bottom (plywood)		¼″ × 3⅜″ × 14¾″	12
Drawer fronts (walnut)		⅝″ × 4½″ × 4½″	12

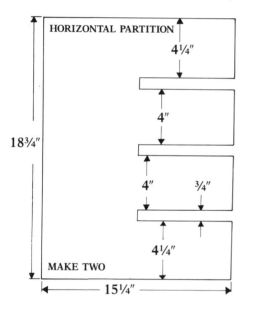

Illus. 32.6   Dimensions for the horizontal partition boards.

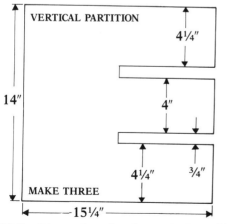

Illus. 32.7   Dimensions for the vertical partition boards.

Basic Cutting for Case

Lay out the horizontal partition (Illus. 32.6) and cut two pieces. Lay out the vertical partition (Illus. 32.7) and cut three pieces. Check the cut size of the partitions and the layout for the slots. Saw the slots out using a band saw or dado blades either on a table saw or with a radial-arm saw. Fit the interlocking parts together.

Cut the sides (Illus. 32.8) and the ends (Illus. 32.9) of the case to size. Lay out and cut the ¾″ dadoes on the table saw or with a radial-arm saw equipped with dado blades. Cut a piece for the back (Illus. 32.10).

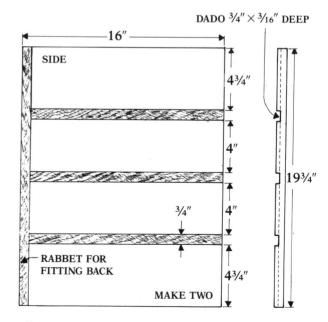

Illus. 32.8   Dimensions for the sides of the case.

118

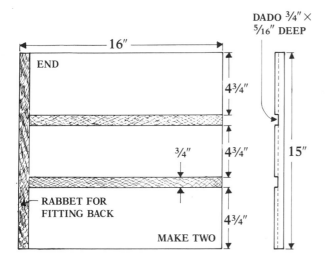

Illus. 32.9   Dimensions for the ends of the case.

Assembly of Case

Assemble the case using screws and covering the screwheads with wood plugs cut from the same material. Sand the plugs flush after the glue has dried. Slide the interlocking partition assembly into the case (Illus. 32.11). The outer edges of each partition slide along a corresponding dado on the inside of the case. Make sure all of the partition boards are flush in the front, and secure the assembly with panelling nails. Set the nail heads below the surface with a nail set.

Cut the facing material to size and sand the edges. Counterbore and drill pilot holes for screws. Assemble the facings over the front edges of the case and partitions with 1″ No. 6 screws. Cover the screwheads with wood plugs. Leave the plugs protruding from the holes to allow them to be sanded flush after the glue dries. Sand all surfaces flush, first with coarse grit garnet paper followed with medium and fine grits.

Basic Cutting for Drawers

Plane and rip material for the sides (Illus. 32.12) and ends (Illus. 32.13) of the drawers. Cut a rabbet along one edge as shown to accommodate the drawer bottom (Illus. 32.14). Cut all parts to size.

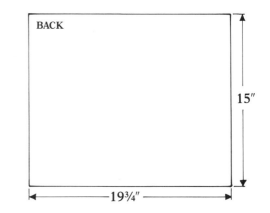

Illus. 32.10   Dimensions for the back.

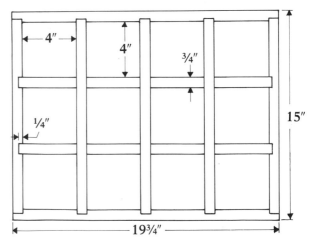

Illus. 32.11   Front view of the addition of the partition assembly inside the outer case.

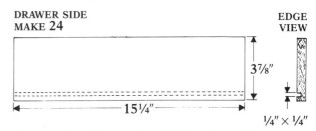

Illus. 32.12   Dimensions for the drawer side.

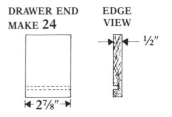

Illus. 32.13   Dimensions for the drawer end.

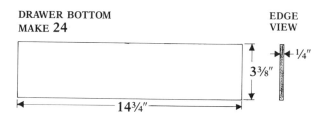

DRAWER BOTTOM
MAKE **24**

EDGE VIEW

3⅜″

¼″

14¾″

Illus. 32.14   Dimensions for the drawer bottom.

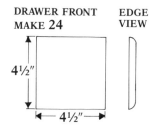

DRAWER FRONT
MAKE **24**

EDGE VIEW

4½″

4½″

Illus. 32.15   Dimensions for the drawer front.

Drawer Assembly

Assemble the drawer box with glue and panelling nails. First, glue and nail the two sides to one end, then slide the bottom board in place. Fasten the remaining end with glue and nails.

Plane and cut the drawer fronts to size (Illus. 32.15), then sand all the edges and front surface. Rout around all four edges with a ¼″ rounding-over bit. Assemble the drawer front to the drawer box by driving screws through one end of the box and into the back of the drawer front. Drill a ³⁄₁₆″ hole in the middle of each drawer front for attaching the knobs.

Finishing

Fine-sand all parts where a finish is to be applied. Remove all dust particles, then apply three coats of satin polyurethane finish to all outside surfaces. Allow each coat to dry according to the manufacturer's directions. Fine-sand between coats with 220-grit garnet paper.

33 ◆ NINETEENTH CENTURY CHEST

This lovely small chest is a replica of a chest that was lent to me by a friend. The original had been in the friend's family since the mid-1800s. They referred to it as a campaign chest, although some chests carried into a campaign by officers were larger, more like portable bureaus or stacked trunks. The chest pictured is made of walnut and has handmade handles. Other hardwoods are suitable, and commercially made handles and latches are readily available.

SUPPLIES

- Saw
- Router
- Plane
- Drill
- Carpenter's glue
- Thirty-six 1¼" No. 8 screws
- Thirty 1" panelling nails
- Garnet paper, 80, 120, and 180 grits
- Semi-gloss polyurethane finish
- Commercially-made hardware, as desired

Materials		Quantity
Sides	¾" × 4⅜" × 16"	2
Ends	¾" × 4⅜" × 6¼"	2
Bottom	¾" × 6¼" × 14½"	1
Lid sides	¾" × 1" × 16"	2
Lid ends	¾" × 2¼" × 6¼"	2
Slats for top	⅜" × 1" × 15¾"	7

INSTRUCTIONS

The construction is straightforward for both the bottom part of the chest and the lid. The ends of the chest fit inside the sides, fastened with lap joints along rabbets prepared in the side pieces. The bottom fits inside the sides and the ends. The lid pieces assemble in the same manner, with a rabbet running along the top edges so that the top slats can be secured and sanded smooth (Illus. 33.1).

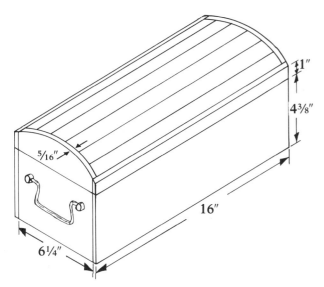

Illus. 33.1 Overall dimensions of chest, showing curved top after slats have been sanded smooth.

121

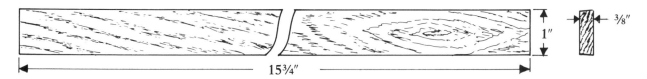

Illus. 33.2 Dimensions for slats. Cut about ¼″ long for later trimming to fit.

Basic Cutting

Plane boards to specified thickness. Following the overall dimensions given (Illus. 33.1), lay out and cut pieces for the sides, ends, and lid sides. From the ⅜″-thick wood cut seven slats (Illus. 33.2), allowing about ¼″ extra length to be trimmed to fit during lid assembly. Lay out the dimensions for the two lid end pieces (Illus. 33.3). Note the dotted lines on the drawings; they indicate that you should leave extra length on the lid ends until the rabbet is routed along the curved edge. The extra length will prevent the router from undercutting at the ends. After the routing is completed, cut the lid ends to the specified length.

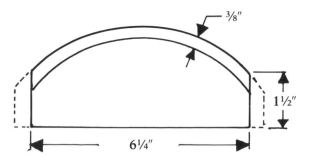

Illus. 33.3 Dimensions for lid end. Dotted lines indicate extra length to be left until rabbet has been routed along the curved edge.

Preparation for Assembly

Cut a rabbet on each end of the sides (Illus. 33.4) to allow the ends to be lap-jointed to the sides. Cut rabbets on the lid sides as well (Illus. 33.5). Drill pilot holes through the slats to prevent the nails from splitting the ends of the slats.

Counterbore and drill holes at all screw locations.

Assembly

Secure the sides to the ends with glue and screws. Glue wood plugs in the counterbored holes to cover the screwheads. After the glue dries, sand the wood plugs flush.

Secure the slats to the lid with glue and 1″ panelling nails. Set the nail heads below the surface with a nail set. After the glue dries, sand the slats to form a smooth rounded surface.

Cut a bottom piece to fit. Secure the bottom inside the ends and sides with glue and screws. Cover the screwheads with wood plugs.

Finishing

Sand all surfaces, first with medium-grit garnet paper, followed with fine grit. Apply a

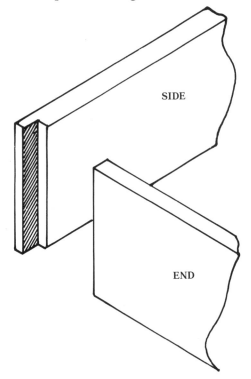

Illus. 33.4 Rabbet cut in side piece to allow end piece to join side with a lap joint. Rabbet on the side piece is ⅜″ × ¾″ to fit the end board.

semi-gloss polyurethane finish according to the manufacturer's directions.

Attaching Hardware

The handles used making the chest pictured were handmade from ⅛″ brass welding rod and buttons turned from walnut stock. Each button has a round tenon turned at the bottom to provide for mounting on the ends of the chest. Commercially-made handles are available as well. Attach brass hinges and snap catches as shown in the photograph.

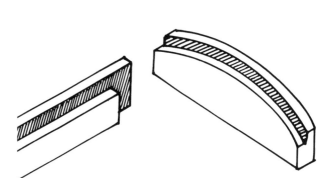

Illus. 33.5   Rabbets along lid side and end pieces to allow the end and side to form a lap joint, and for fitting and securing the top slats.

34 ◆ PIE SAFE

This handsome pie safe no longer need be confined to the kitchen or pantry. Its friendly familiarity reminds us that "everything old is new again." In years past the pie safe was used, as the name implies, to store the many pies baked for the household. Today the pie safe can be used for linens, china, or the stereo system, perhaps even for a medium-sized television with the removal of the top shelf.

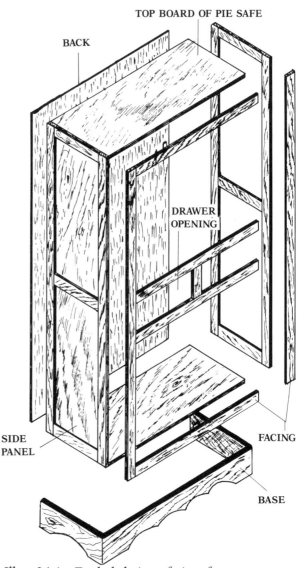

TOP BOARD OF PIE SAFE

BACK

DRAWER OPENING

SIDE PANEL

FACING

BASE

Illus. 34.1   Exploded view of pie safe case assembly (without shelves), and base assembly.

INSTRUCTIONS

The construction of the pie safe will take some time, but it is quite straightforward. There are five basic elements or assemblies that are constructed separately, and then put together to form the completed piece; these elements are not equal in size or complexity. The first element is the case assembly (Illus. 34.1) which sits on top of the base assembly. The case assembly includes the back, side panels, facing, top and bottom boards, the middle drawer-support shelf and second middle shelf (Illus. 34.2), and the top and bottom shelves (Illus. 34.3).

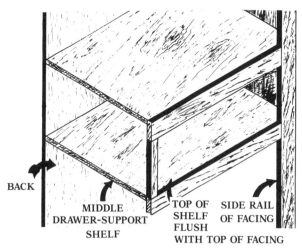

Illus. 34.2   Cutaway view of middle drawer-support shelf and second middle shelf construction details.

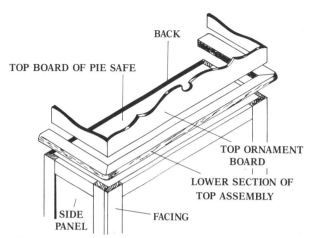

Illus. 34.4   Exploded view of ornamental top assembly.

Illus. 34.3   View of top shelf and second middle shelf, which serves as the bottom of the top compartment in the finished pie safe cabinet.

Illus. 34.5   Tooling tin panel to form design for doors by tapping the point of a nail through the tin, following pattern.

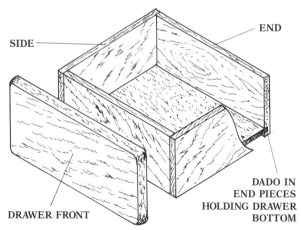

Illus. 34.6   Drawer assembly showing cutaway view of drawer bottom construction and exploded view of drawer front.

The remaining elements are the ornamental top assembly (Illus. 34.4), the four doors which require the tooling of tin panels (Illus. 34.5), and the two drawers (Illus. 34.6).

125

Materials			Quantity
Case assembly:	Side panels	$3/4'' \times 1\,7/8'' \times 56''$	4
		$3/4'' \times 1\,7/8'' \times 11''$	6
		$1/2'' \times 12'' \times 26''$	4
	Bottom, top, shelves	$3/4'' \times 13'' \times 36''$	6
	Facing	$3/4'' \times 1\,7/8'' \times 56''$	2
		$3/4'' \times 1\,7/8'' \times 36''$	4
		$3/4'' \times 1\,7/8'' \times 7''$	1
	Support strips	$3/4'' \times 3/4'' \times 13''$	8
	Back board	$3/4'' \times 36'' \times 56''$	1
Base assembly:	Front	$3/4'' \times 5\,1/2'' \times 38\,3/8''$	1
	Sides	$3/4'' \times 5\,1/2'' \times 15\,1/2''$	2
Ornamental top assembly:	Front	$3/4'' \times 5'' \times 37''$	1
	Sides	$3/4'' \times 5'' \times 14''$	2
Lower section of top:	Front	$1\,1/4'' \times 4'' \times 38\,1/2''$	1
	Sides	$1\,1/4'' \times 4'' \times 16''$	2
Door frames:	Side frames	$3/4'' \times 1\,7/8'' \times 22''$	8
	Top/bottom frames	$3/4'' \times 1\,7/8'' \times 16''$	8
	Wood strips	$1/4'' \times 3/4'' \times 20''$	8
		$1/4'' \times 3/4'' \times 16''$	8
Drawer box:	Sides	$3/4'' \times 6\,1/4'' \times 13''$	4
	Ends	$3/4'' \times 6\,1/4'' \times 15\,11/16''$	4
	Bottoms	$1/4'' \times 13'' \times 14\,7/8''$	2
Drawer front:		$3/4'' \times 7\,3/4'' \times 17\,3/16''$	2
Tin for decorative panels		$16'' \times 20''$	4

Constructing the Case Assembly

Rip stock to width, allowing extra to be removed during finishing. Smooth the edges with a jointer. Lay out pieces for the side panel frames (Illus. 34.7). Cut all parts to length. Mark the location of dowel holes at each joint. Drill the holes, and assemble the frames with glue and dowels (Illus. 34.8).

Clamp the panel frames with pipe clamps. Sand the front and back surfaces flush. Rout a $3/8''$ radius around the top inside edge of the frame. Rout a rabbet on the back inside edge to accommodate the $3/8''$-thick panels (Illus. 34.9). Cut panels to fit. Solid yellow pine was used for the pie safe pictured, but plywood may be used as well. Fine-sand the surfaces of the panel. Secure the panels in the frames with wire brads.

Lay out pieces for the top and bottom boards, and for the four shelves. Cut the boards to width $1/2''$ less than the sides of the pie safe case. Glue and dowel narrower boards edgewise to obtain the necessary width. All six boards should be identical in width and length.

Prepare for assembling the side panels, and bottom and top boards by cutting a rabbet, $3/8'' \times 1/2''$, along the inside back edge of each side panel (Illus. 34.10). Counterbore a $3/8'' \times 3/8''$ hole for each screw.

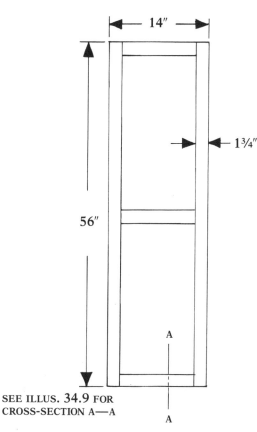

SEE ILLUS. **34.9** FOR
CROSS-SECTION A—A

Illus. 34.7   Dimensions for side panel frames.

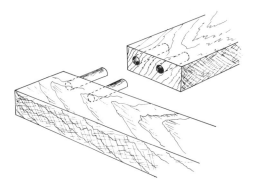

Illus. 34.8   Dowelling a butt joint for frames and facing.

Attach the top and bottom boards between the side panels (Illus. 34.1). Each board should be flush with the front edges of the side panels, and also flush with the back of the rabbet—½" inset from the back edge of the panels. Secure wood plugs in the counterbored holes with glue. Sand the wood plugs flush after the glue dries.

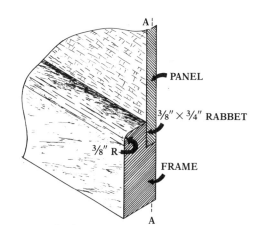

Illus. 34.9   Detail of panel construction showing cross-section A—A of Illus. 34.7.

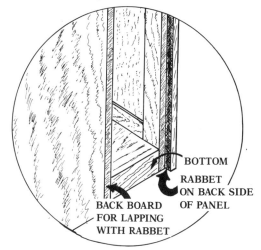

Illus. 34.10   Detail of back and bottom construction showing joint with rabbeted side panel.

SUPPLIES

- ¾" brads
- No. 16 nails
- Screws and wood plugs
- Table saw
- Jointer
- Drill
- Router, ⅜" bits
- Clamps
- Garnet paper of various grits
- Mallet
- Duct tape
- Stain and finish, as desired
- Four cabinet hinges, ¾" offset, spring-loaded
- Eight 1" porcelain knobs

Lay out pieces for the facing (Illus. 34.11). Cut all parts to length, and smooth all of the edges on the jointer. Mark the location of dowel holes. Glue and dowel the facing frame, and then clamp with pipe clamps. Sand the back and front surfaces after the glue dries. Attach the facing frame to the front of the pie safe case assembly with screws. Cover the screws with the wood plugs, and sand after the glue dries.

Prepare for installing the shelves by cutting support strips, ¾″ × ¾″ × 13″. Fasten the strips for the middle drawer-support shelf so that the shelf will be flush with the bottom of the drawer opening (Illus. 34.2). The remaining shelves don't require permanent support strips, but you can install them if you wish or use them only for proper placement. The second middle shelf should be flush with the top of the facing just above the drawer opening. This shelf serves as the bottom of the top cabinet compartment (Illus. 34.3).

The back board should be ½″ thick and can be made of two or more boards rabbeted along the edges so they overlap to form a lap joint when secured in place. Cut pieces for the back allowing enough length so that each board extends fully behind the top and bottom boards. Fasten with screws.

Attaching the Base Assembly

Enlarge the pattern for the front base piece to full size using a one-inch grid (Illus. 34.12). Cut parts for the base to length (Illus. 34.13), and sand all surfaces. Secure base assembly with screws and fasten to the bottom of the case assembly. Cover screws with wood plugs. Sand the plugs flush after the glue dries.

Adding the Ornamental Top Assembly

Enlarge the pattern for the scroll design of the front top piece by using a one-inch grid (Illus. 34.14). Cut parts for the ornamental top to shape (Illus. 34.15). Assemble the lower section to the top of the pie safe case assembly with screws as shown in the inset cross section A—A in Illus. 34.15. Then attach the top ornamental boards to the lower section of the top assembly (Illus. 34.4).

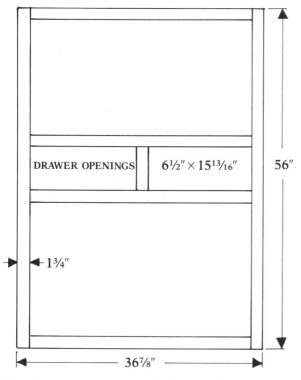

DRAWER OPENINGS | 6½″ × 15¹³⁄₁₆″

56″

1¾″

36⅞″

Illus. 34.11 Dimensions for facing of case assembly.

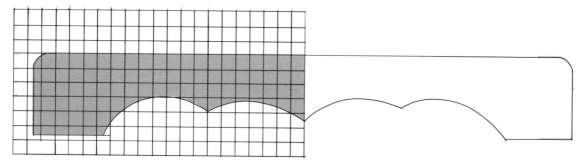

Illus. 34.12 Pattern for front base piece. For full-size pattern, enlarge on a 1″ grid.

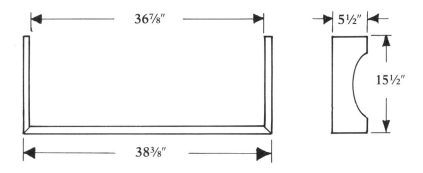

Illus. 34.13   Dimensions for base assembly.

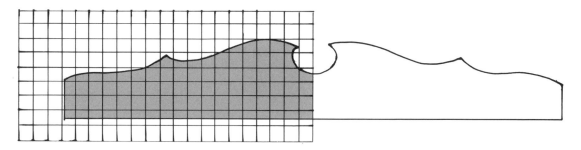

Illus. 34.14   Pattern for scroll design of front top piece. For full-size pattern, enlarge on a 1" grid.

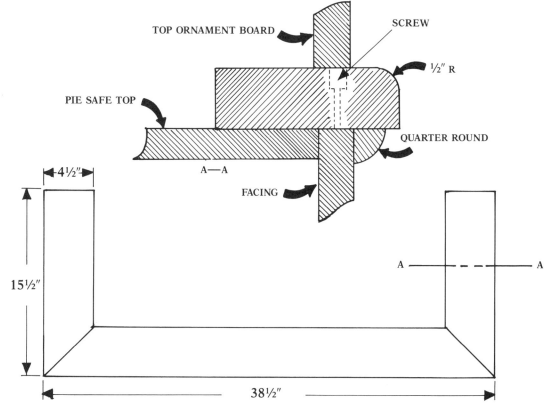

Illus. 34.15   Dimensions for lower section of top assembly, with construction detail showing cross section of top assembly and pie safe top.

Assembling Tin-Panelled Doors

Lay out pieces for the four doors (Illus. 34.16). Cut the parts to length, and smooth the edges on a jointer. Mark locations for dowels on each piece. Drill the dowel holes, and then assemble the door frames with glue and dowels. Clamp with pipe clamps. Sand the front and back surfaces flush.

Rout a ⅜" radius around the inside front edges, and then rout a ¼" rabbet around the inside back edges (Illus. 34.17). Rout around the outside front edges with a ⅜" ogee bit. Fine-sand all surfaces.

Prepare to tool the panels for the doors by enlarging the design to full size on a one-inch grid (Illus. 34.18). Make two piercing tools from No. 16 common nails; one nail should be sharper than the other for making smaller holes in the more delicate parts of the design. The blunt tool will make the bigger holes along the borders.

Transfer the design to heavy paper and tape the design over the surface of the tin. Tape the edges of the tin to a plywood board. Tool the panels by tapping the point of the piercing tool through the tin using a mallet. Keep the strokes even, and space the point of the tool evenly along the lines of the design.

Fasten the completed design inside the door frame with wood strips, ¼" × ¾" (Illus. 34.17). Secure the strips with wire brads.

Attach the completed door assemblies to the front of the pie safe assembly. Fasten the doors using standard ¾" offset, spring-loaded cabinet hinges (Illus. 34.3).

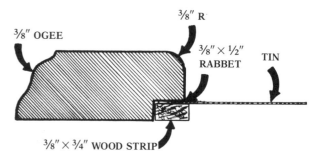
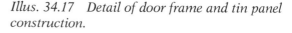

Illus. 34.17   Detail of door frame and tin panel construction.

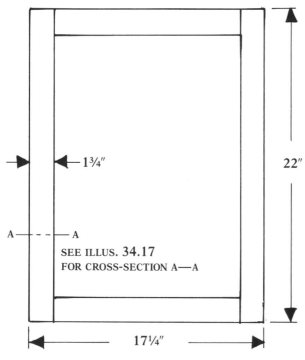

Illus. 34.16   Dimensions for door frames.

130

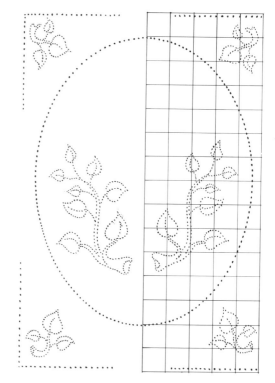

Illus. 34.18   Pattern for tooled-tin panels in doors. For full-size pattern, enlarge on a 1" grid.

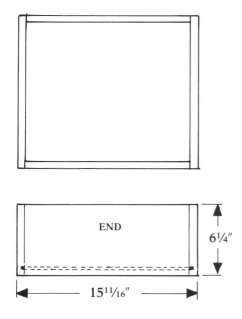

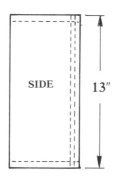

SIDE 13″

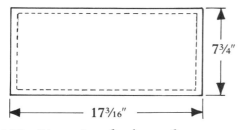

END

6¼″

15¹¹⁄₁₆″

Illus. 34.19   Dimensions for drawer box.

7¾″

17³⁄₁₆″

Illus. 34.20   Dimensions for drawer front.

Constructing the Drawers

Cut materials to shape (Illus. 34.19). Sand all surfaces. Cut pieces for the drawer fronts (Illus. 34.20), and sand all surfaces.

Assemble the drawer parts with glue and screws (Illus. 34.6). Fit the drawers in the pie safe. Attach wood strips on the bottom of the drawer carriage to hold the drawer straight as it slides in and out.

Finishing

Apply stain, as desired. Follow the manufacturer's directions. You may consider sealing the wood with polyurethane finish.

Garden, Patio, and Workshop Furnishings

35 ◆ DEACON'S BENCH

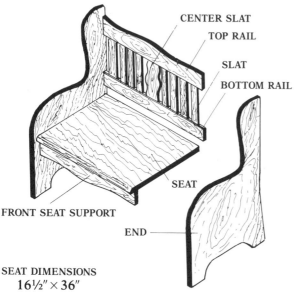

CENTER SLAT

TOP RAIL

SLAT

BOTTOM RAIL

SEAT

FRONT SEAT SUPPORT

END

SEAT DIMENSIONS
16½″ × 36″

Illus. 35.1   Exploded view of deacon's bench, showing parts.

This sturdy oak bench will enhance the comfortable, country look of your home whether you place it in the entranceway or on the patio, or along a garden path. Suitably finished, this bench serves equally well outdoors or in.

SUPPLIES

- Twelve 2″ No. 10 flat-head screws
- 1″ wire brads
- Table saw or radial-arm saw
- Dado blades
- Planer
- Jointer
- Band saw
- Drill, with ⅜″ boring bit, ⅛″ twist drill
- Carpenter's glue
- Garnet paper, various grits
- Router, with ⅜″ and ¼″ rounding-over bits
- Stain, as desired
- Polyurethane finish or tung oil varnish, as desired

INSTRUCTIONS

The deacon's bench is not complicated to construct, but, because of the width of some pieces, you will have to glue up narrower oak boards using dowels and glue. In addition to hidden seat support pieces running along either end, the bench is made up of seven basic pieces (Illus. 35.1). Construction proceeds in four stages: the ends are glued up and cut; the back assembly is put together; the seat assembly is readied; and finally the back and seat assemblies are attached to the ends.

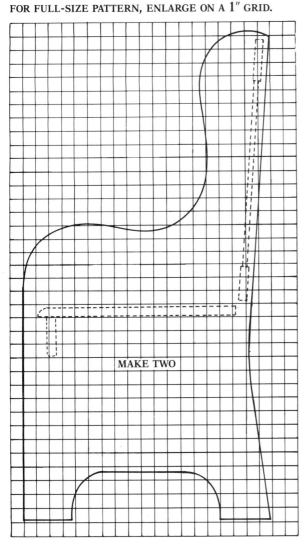

MAKE TWO

Illus. 35.2   Pattern for ends.

Cutting the Ends

Cut boards to rough dimensions and smooth edges on the jointer. Lay the boards edge-to-edge and mark the location of dowel holes. Drill the dowel holes. Add glue, then tap dowel pins into the holes. Assemble the boards, clamping the edges together. After the glue is dry, sand the surfaces flush.

Enlarge the pattern for the ends to full size (Illus. 35.2) and transfer to the wood. Use a band saw to saw the glued-up end pieces to shape. Sand the edges smooth and rout a ¼″ radius around all edges with rounding-over bit. Sand surfaces with medium-grit garnet paper followed by fine grit.

Constructing the Back Assembly

Cut boards for the top and bottom rails (Illus. 35.3) to rough length, leaving about one inch extra for trimming later. Enlarge the pattern to full size for cutting the curved lines along the top rail. Transfer the pattern to the wood, then cut the pattern with a band saw. Cut a ½″ by ½″ dado down a straight edge along both rails (Illus. 35.4).

Prepare boards for making the slats by planing material to a ½″ thickness. Cut the center slat and the ten straight slats to size (Illus. 35.5). Smooth the edges of the straight slats on a jointer. Cut the center slat on a band saw. Rout along the edges of each board using a ¼″ rounding-over bit. Sand all surfaces as needed.

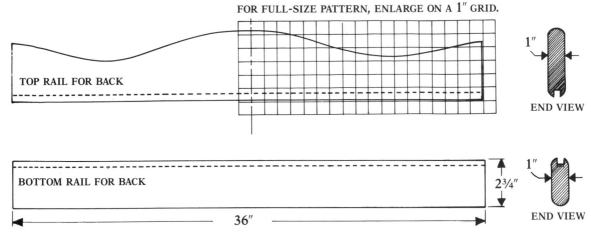

TOP RAIL FOR BACK

1″

END VIEW

BOTTOM RAIL FOR BACK

36″

1″

2¾″

END VIEW

Illus. 35.3   Dimensions for the top and bottom rail.

Materials		Quantity
Ends (glued-up oak)	$13/16'' \times 19'' \times 36''$	2
Top rail	$1'' \times 5\frac{1}{2}'' \times 36''$	1
Bottom rail	$1'' \times 2\frac{3}{4}'' \times 36''$	1
Center slat	$\frac{1}{2}'' \times 5'' \times 12''$	1
Straight slats	$\frac{1}{2}'' \times 2\frac{1}{2}'' \times 12''$	10
Front seat support	$1'' \times 5\frac{1}{2}'' \times 36''$	1
Hidden seat support	$1'' \times 2'' \times 15''$	2
Seat (glued-up oak)	$\frac{3}{4}'' \times 16\frac{1}{2}'' \times 36''$	1

Preparing the Seat Assembly

Cut boards to rough length and glue up in the same manner as for the end pieces. Cut the seat piece to size, 16½" by 36". Cut the front seat support (Illus. 35.7) to a 36" length. Cut the support to shape with a band saw. Sand the glued-up seat boards flush and fine-sand. Rout along the front edge of the seat and along the curved edge of the front seat support using a ¼" rounding-over bit.

Cut the two small boards to be used as hidden support pieces (Illus. 35.8). Drill and countersink screw holes in the two hidden support pieces.

Cut the top and bottom rails to their exact length of 36". Cut spacer blocks to fit in the dadoes on the top and bottom rails using the same material as that used for making the slats (Illus. 35.6). Start putting the spacer blocks and slats together for final assembly by first gluing and clamping one end slat in place. Drill a ¹⁄₁₆" hole through each spacer block. Assemble the remaining slats by placing spacer blocks at top and bottom. Secure each spacer block with a small amount of glue and a wire brad through the prepared hole. The last pair of spacer blocks might need slight altering to provide a proper fit for the last slat. The outside slats should be flush with the ends of the top and bottom rails. Secure the slats in place with additional furniture clamps until the glue is dry.

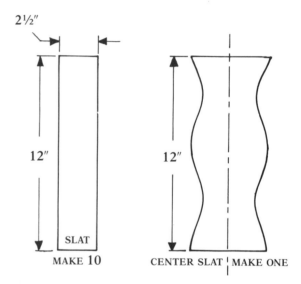

Illus. 35.5   Dimensions for center slat and straight slats.

Illus. 35.4   Dadoes cut along top and bottom rails.

Illus. 35.6   Detail of spacer blocks being fitted in dado of bottom rail.

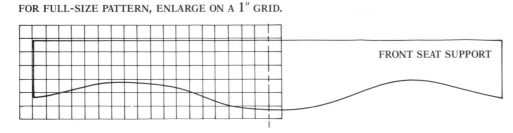

Illus. 35.7   Pattern for front seat support.

Attaching Back and Seat Assemblies to the Ends

Locate the hidden support pieces on the inside surface of the end pieces. Secure the hidden support pieces in place with screws. Mark the locations for mounting the back assembly and the front seat support to the ends (Illus. 35.2). Counterbore a ⅜″ by ⅜″ hole at each screw location, then drill a pilot hole through the remaining board thickness.

Clamp the back assembly and front seat support in place with furniture clamps. Secure the boards to the ends with screws. Glue wood plugs to cover the screws, and sand them flush after the glue is dry.

Place the seat between the two ends and on top of the hidden support pieces. Check the fit, making adjustments as needed so that the seat fits comfortably and squarely in place. Secure the seat by driving screws through the pilot holes in the two hidden support pieces (Illus. 35.9).

Finishing

If stain is used, apply according to manufacturer's directions and allow it to dry for at least eight hours. Fine-sand lightly with 220-grit paper, then wipe all dust from the wood. Apply a polyurethane finish or a tung oil varnish, as desired, sanding lightly between coats with the 220-grit paper. Allow sufficient drying time between coats.

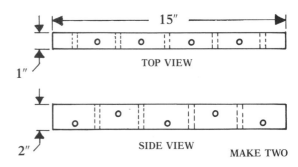

Illus. 35.8   Dimensions for hidden seat support pieces, showing location of sites for securing screws.

Illus. 35.9   Detail of hidden support piece with screws in place.

36 ◆ PLANTER CART

This natural cedar cart is a delightful gift for the gardener in your house or for a gardening friend. Any occasion—Mother's Day, Father's Day, or the first day of spring—is appropriate for making a gift of your handiwork. The cedar wood planter is quick to build and accommodates at least two potted plants for indoor or outdoor decoration. An informal arrangement of fruit or homegrown vegetables is equally appealing.

SUPPLIES

- Saw, with mitre gauge
- Drill
- Ten 1¼″ No. 8 hardboard screws
- Forty-eight 2d common galvanized nails
- ½″ diameter dowel
- ³⁄₁₆″ diameter dowel
- ⅛″ diameter dowel
- Sandpaper, various grits

INSTRUCTIONS

The planter cart construction is straightforward (Illus. 36.1), only requiring a saw and a drill in terms of special tools. The only pieces needing extra care are the ends (Illus. 36.2), which require a compound angle to be cut (instructions are provided). The wood is left unpainted to allow the natural color and texture of the cedar to add to the rustic appeal of the planter.

Basic Cutting

The end pieces (Illus. 36.2) join the bottom with a slope of 18 degrees (Illus. 36.3). Begin by cutting a piece for the bottom. Cut the 18 degree angle on either end of the bottom piece—and along both edges.

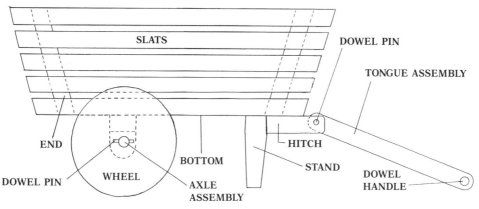

Illus. 36.1   Planter cart assembly, showing parts.

136

Materials		Quantity
Bottom	¾″ × 5½″ × 9½″	1
Ends	¾″ × 5½″ × 8″	2
Slats (cut to length)	³⁄₁₆″ × ¾″ × 15″	10
Wheels (cut to size)	¾″ × 5½″ × 5½″	2
Axle assembly	¾″ × 2″ × 7″	1
Stand	¾″ × 2½″ × 4″	1
Hitch	¾″ × 2½″ × 4¼″	1
Tongue	¾″ × 1¼″ × 9½″	1

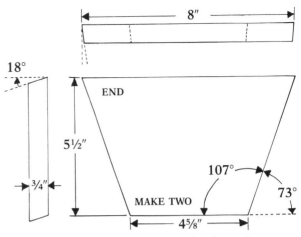

Illus. 36.2   Dimensions and angles for end pieces.

Lay out the dimensions for the end pieces. In addition to the end pieces joining the bottom piece flush at the 18 degree angle, the ends are cut to allow the sides to slope at 18 degrees as well. The result is a compound angle on the end pieces. Cut the compound angle on each end piece by first tilting the saw blade to 5¼ degrees from its normal 90 degree setting. Next, set the mitre gauge on 73 degrees. Now you can make the side cuts.

The bottom and top edges of the end pieces are cut at the simple angle of 18 degrees—as were the edges and ends of the bottom piece.

Cut pieces for the ten slats (Illus. 36.4), cutting two for each of the dimensions given. Cut out two pieces for the wheels (Illus. 36.5), and drill a ½″ hole in the middle of each wheel, as shown. Cut pieces for the axle assembly (Illus.

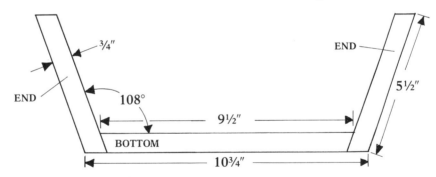

Illus. 36.3   End and bottom assembly, showing dimensions and angle.

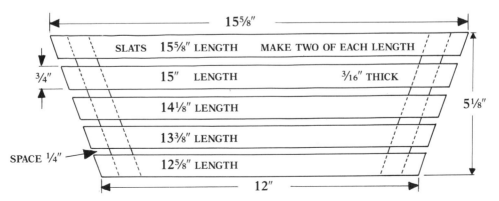

Illus. 36.4   Dimension for slats and slat assembly to ends.

137

36.6), including the ½" by ½" dowel for the axles. Drill ½" holes to accommodate the axles. Drill a 3⁄16" hole in each axle to accommodate the wheel-retaining dowel pins.

Cut pieces for the stand and the hitch (Illus. 36.7). Drill a 1⁄8" hole through the hitch to accommodate the dowel pin for attaching the tongue. Cut a piece for the tongue (Illus. 36.8),

and drill a 1⁄8" hole for the attaching dowel pin. Also drill a 3⁄16" hole to accommodate the dowel handle.

Counterbore holes in the axle assembly piece, the stand, and the hitch, as shown on the plans. Drill pilot holes for the screw shanks through the remaining thickness.

Sand all surfaces as required.

Assembly

Glue the axle dowel pieces into the axle assembly. Secure the ends to the bottom, then attach

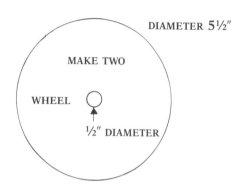

Illus. 36.5 Dimensions for wheels.

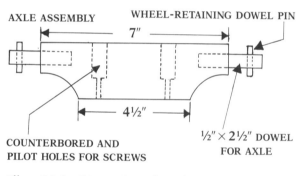

Illus. 36.6 Dimensions for axle assembly.

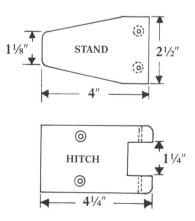

Illus. 36.7 Dimensions for stand and hitch.

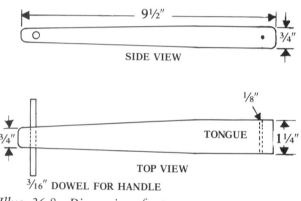

Illus. 36.8 Dimensions for tongue.

Illus. 36.9 Attaching axle assembly to bottom of cart with screws.

138

the ten slats to form both sides of the planter cart (Illus. 36.4). Attach the axle assembly to the bottom of the cart (Illus. 36.9).

Attach the stand to the hitch, then install the tongue assembly (Illus. 36.10). Using screws, secure the hitch, stand, and tongue assembly to the bottom of the cart. Attach the wheels by securing them with the wheel-retaining dowels.

Finishing

There is no finishing necessary, except sanding the ends of the slats with a sanding block, and any other sanding desired.

Illus. 36.10   Putting together the tongue assembly with the hitch and stand assembly.

This cozy wide-backed Adirondack chair harks back to the days of the great country inns, but its popularity may never have been greater. The chair pictured is painted in a contemporary color (see the color section) and would suit a patio or deck, the garden or lawn, or a setup at the beach. The material used is C-grade or clear yellow pine.

Materials		Quantity
Rear leg and		
seat boards	3/4″ × 6¼″ × 37″	2
Arms	3/4″ × 5½″ × 25½″	2
Front legs	3/4″ × 4¾″ × 21¼″	2
Arm supports	3/4″ × 3″ × 12″	2
Seat slats	3/4″ × 1¼″ × 19¼″	13
Center back piece	3/4″ × 9″ × 40″	1
Outer back pieces	3/4″ × 2½″ × 40″	4
Middle		
cross-member	3/4″ × 2″ × 24″	1
Lower		
cross-member	3/4″ × 2″ × 17″	1
Spacer boards	3/4″ × 4½″ × 17¾″	2

INSTRUCTIONS

The construction of the chair requires simple tools such as a saw and a drill; the only specialty tool is a pipe or bar clamp. The design of the chair lends itself to building several chairs at once. A feature of the construction is that chairs can be built in two main assemblies—the back assembly, and the rear legs-and-seat assembly—and then combined with the arm and front leg pieces in a swift procedure (Illus. 37.1).

Basic Cutting

Enlarge the patterns for the rear leg and seat board (Illus. 37.2) and for the arm (Illus. 37.3) to full size. Cut pieces for the front legs (Illus. 37.4), for the arm supports (Illus. 37.5), and for the thirteen seat slats (Illus. 37.6).

SUPPLIES

- Forty-eight 1¼″ No. 8 hardboard screws
- Four ¼″ by 2″ carriage bolts
- Saw
- Pipe or bar clamp
- Drill
- String and nail
- Carpenter's glue
- Sandpaper, various grits
- Paint or finish, as desired

Cut all the parts to shape for the back assembly (Illus. 37.7), but do not cut the rounded top on the boards for the back of the chair. This will be done after the back has been assembled.

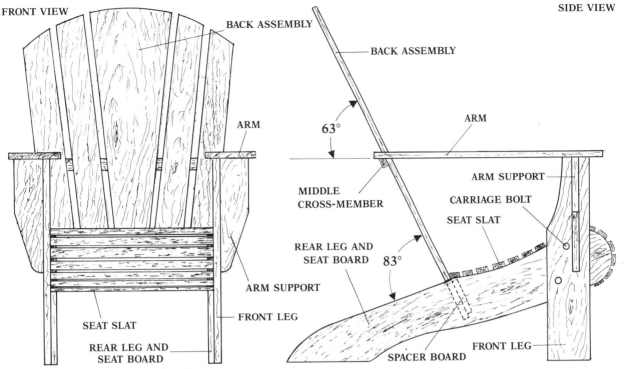

FRONT VIEW

SIDE VIEW

BACK ASSEMBLY

BACK ASSEMBLY

ARM

63°

ARM

MIDDLE
CROSS-MEMBER

ARM SUPPORT

CARRIAGE BOLT

SEAT SLAT

REAR LEG AND
SEAT BOARD

83°

ARM SUPPORT

FRONT LEG

SEAT SLAT

REAR LEG AND
SEAT BOARD

FRONT LEG

SPACER BOARD

Illus. 37.1   Adirondack chair, showing parts.

REAR LEG AND SEAT BOARD   FOR FULL-SIZE PATTERN, ENLARGE ON 1″ GRID.

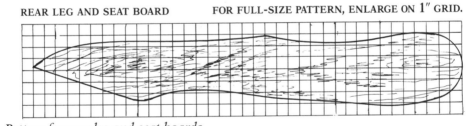

Illus. 37.2   Pattern for rear leg and seat boards.

ARM   FOR FULL-SIZE PATTERN, ENLARGE ON A 1″ GRID.

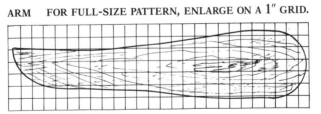

Illus. 37.3   Pattern for arm.

FRONT LEG   MAKE TWO

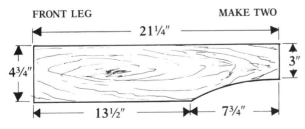

21¼″

3″

4¾″

13½″   7¾″

Illus. 37.4   Dimensions for front leg.

ARM SUPPORT   MAKE TWO

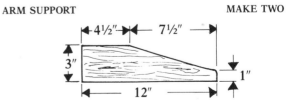

4½″   7½″

3″

1″

12″

Illus. 37.5   Dimensions for arm support.

141

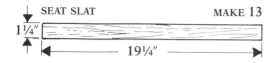

SEAT SLAT   MAKE 13

1¼"

19¼"

Illus. 37.6   Dimensions for seat slat.

Back Assembly

Lay the back assembly parts on a flat surface, and place ¾" spacer blocks between the boards. Clamp the blocks in place using a bar or pipe clamp (Illus. 37.8). While the back parts remain clamped, measure and secure the cross-members. The middle cross-member extends out from the sides for fastening the arms to the back. Other cross-member ends are sawed off flush with the edges of the back.

To round the top of the back assembly, fasten a string to a pencil and secure the other end to a small nail placed 13" above the bottom at midpoint of its width. The point of the pencil should be about 32" from the bottom

Illus. 37.8   Using pipe clamp and spacer blocks to assemble back. Cross-members are secured with glue and screws.

directly above the nail, so that the distance between the nail and the pencil is about 19". Scribe a line with the pencil in a smooth arc to mark the rounded top (Illus. 37.9). Cut along the curved line to form the top edge of the back assembly.

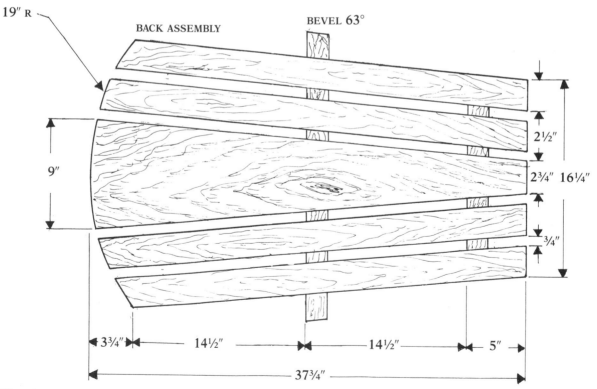

19" R

BACK ASSEMBLY   BEVEL 63°

9"

2½"

2¾"   16¼"

¾"

3¾"   14½"   14½"   5"

37¾"

Illus. 37.7   Dimensions for back assembly.

142

Rear Leg-and-Seat Assembly

Lay out the locations for the inside spacer boards. Cut the spacer boards 4½″ high and 17¾″ long. The angle of the back spacer board will determine the angle of the back (Illus. 37.1). Secure the spacer boards between the sides of the rear leg and seat board (Illus. 37.10).

Drill and countersink holes on each of the slats to accommodate screws. Attach the seat slats, spacing the slats ½″ apart. A ½″ strip of scrap wood is useful as a gauge for spacing the slats. You may not need all thirteen slats. Sand the ends of the slats flush with the surface of the seat base.

Combining Assemblies with Front Legs and Arms

Fasten the bottom of the back assembly to the inside spacer board with screws (Illus. 37.11). Attach the front legs with carriage bolts (Illus. 37.1). Position the arms on the front legs and on the middle cross-member (Illus. 37.12). Secure the arms with screws. Using glue and screws, fasten the arm supports to the front legs and arms.

Paint or finish as desired.

Illus. 37.11   Bottom of back assembly is fastened to the inside spacer board with screws.

Illus. 37.9   After assembly a string and pencil are used to mark rounded top of back.

Illus. 37.10   Spacer boards are secured between sides of seat.

Illus. 37.12   Final assembly is accomplished by arranging arm piece to be fastened to the top of front leg and to middle cross-member of the back assembly.

This stencilled flower box with legs is just right for the patio or for decorating a porch. Leave off the legs and the flower box becomes a traditional window box placed on the sill. The flower box pictured is made of white pine, but you may use any of many suitable woods.

SUPPLIES

- Thirty-six 1¼″ No. 9 sheetrock screws
- Table saw
- Scroll saw
- Router, with ⅜″ rounding-over bit
- Garnet paper, 80, 120, and 180 grit
- Polyurethane varnish

INSTRUCTIONS

The construction of the flower box is very straightforward. The assembly consists of a basic box (Illus. 38.1) to which the handle ends and feet are attached. Cutting the stencil is simple—the pattern is traced onto Mylar, with a separate stencil made for each color.

Materials		Quantity
Bottom	¾″ × 5″ × 28½″	1
Sides	¾″ × 7¼″ × 28½″	2
Inner end supports	¾″ × 6″ × 7″	2
Handle ends	¾″ × 9″ × 10¼″	2
Feet	¾″ × 1⅞″ × 9¼″	2

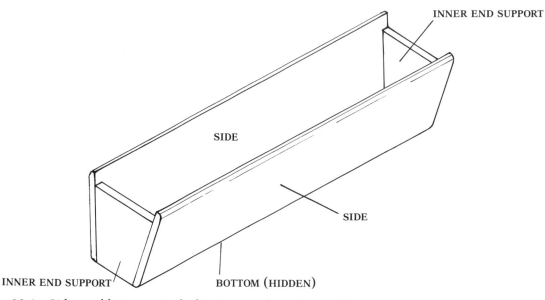

INNER END SUPPORT

SIDE

SIDE

INNER END SUPPORT

BOTTOM (HIDDEN)

Illus. 38.1   Sides and bottom attached to inner end supports with screws.

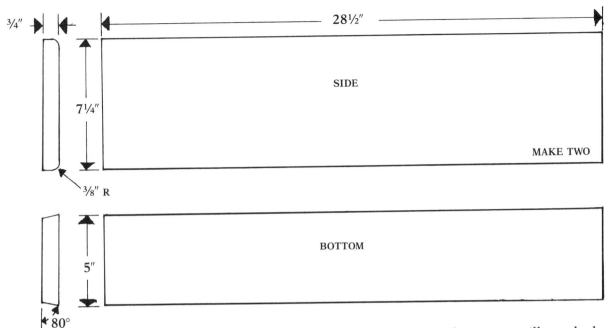

Illus. 38.2   Dimensions of sides and bottom.

Basic Cutting

Cut pieces for the bottom and the two sides (Illus. 38.2). Cut the long edges of the bottom piece at an 80 degree angle. Rout the long edges of the side pieces with a ⅜″ rounding-over bit on one side. Cut two pieces for the inner end supports (Illus. 38.3).

Cut pieces for the two handle ends (Illus. 38.4). Use a scroll saw to cut the openings for the handles. Rout all of the edges except the bottom edge with a ⅜″ rounding-over bit. Cut two pieces for the feet (Illus. 38.5), and rout all

edges except where the pieces will touch the bottom of the flower box and where the feet will sit on the floor. Use the ⅜″ rounding-over router bit.

Assembly

Attach the sides to the bottom, and then fasten the two inside end supports with screws. Fasten the handle ends to the assembled box with

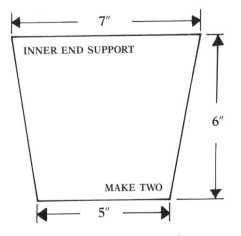

Illus. 38.3   Dimensions of inner end support.

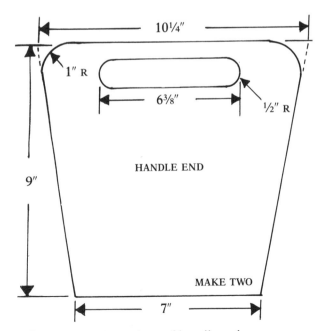

Illus. 38.4   Dimensions of handle end.

screws. Counterbore each screw hole ⅜" by ⅜" through half of the thickness. Drill a ³⁄₁₆" pilot hole through the remaining thickness. Locate the screws so that they are driven into the ends of the sides and the ends of the bottom piece to prevent the sides from pulling apart. Cover the screws with wood plugs, and after the glue dries, sand the plugs flush.

Measure three inches in from either end of the box, and attach the two feet pieces to the bottom with screws.

Stencilling by Zula Erickson

Sand all surfaces with medium-grit garnet paper followed by fine grit. Wipe with a tack cloth to remove dust. Prepare stain and stain the box. Allow the box to dry thoroughly. Paint the inside of the box with a blue acrylic paint, and let dry.

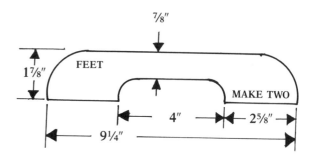

Illus. 38.5   Dimensions of feet to be placed on bottom of box 3" from each end.

Prepare the stencils by tracing the pattern (Illus. 38.6) onto Mylar. Make a separate stencil for each color. Allow at least a one-inch border around any stencil cutout. The dashed lines on the pattern are meant to assist with the placement of the stencils on the flower box.

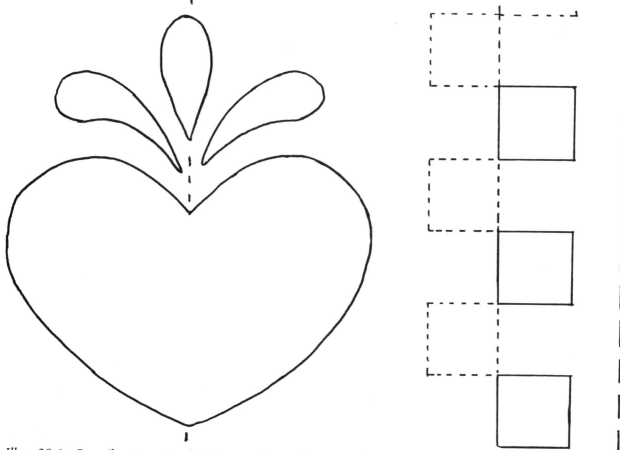

Illus. 38.6   Stencil pattern. Dashed lines are for guiding stencil location on flower box.

146

STENCILLING SUPPLIES

- Mylar, 9″ × 12″
- Stencilling brushes, one for each color
- Foam brush
- Paper towels
- Tack cloth
- Mineral spirits
- Stain
- Blue acrylic paint
- Stencilling paints, colors as desired

Cut the stencils out by placing them flat on a glass surface. Cut along the solid lines.

The checker pattern is placed along the sides using the long dashed line as a guide; the dashed line is placed on the bottom edge of the sides. The short dashed line on the heart stencil helps keep the stencil vertical. Place the stencil you are working with in the correct position, and tape it in place with masking tape.

Review the manufacturer's directions for the paint you will be using. Place a small amount of paint on a palette or in a foil pan. Dip the tip of the brush into the paint. Wipe off the excess on a paper towel until the brush is "dry" and the paint is both light and smooth in appearance. Hold the brush perpendicular to the surface being stencilled. Start at the outside edge of the cut-out area, and work from the edge out over the design area, circling the brush in a clockwise motion.

Now reverse to a counterclockwise motion, and continue building up the color to the desired shade. A "properly" stencilled design element is dark around the edge and lighter toward the middle.

Align the second design element over the previously stencilled area by using the dashed lines. Change to a clean brush when changing colors. Stencil the second element. Continue in this manner until the design has been completed.

Clean brushes and stencils according to the type of paint used and the manufacturer's directions. Allow the brushes to air-dry before using them again.

Finishing
Allow the paint to thoroughly "cure" for at least a full week; then apply several protective coats of a polyurethane varnish.

39 ◆ PORCH OR GARDEN SWING

Here is an old-time fixture of the country home that will bring enjoyment to friends and family. You can hang the porch swing from the porch ceiling as in earlier times. But if you would prefer being able to move the swing to any location on the lawn or near the garden, the plans for a double A-frame swing support are included.

SUPPLIES

- Band saw or jigsaw
- Table saw
- Router, with ¼" rounding-over bit
- Drill
- Sandpaper, various grits
- Finish, as desired

INSTRUCTIONS

The construction of the swing itself involves three steps. First the frame for the seat is assembled, followed by the attaching of the slats. Then the arm assembly, which supports the swing when it is hung, is attached. Once the swing is assembled, the swing support frame is constructed, if desired.

Materials		Quantity
Swing (yellow pine)		
Seat frame ribs	¾" × 3½" × 20"	4
Back of seat frame	¾" × 3½" × 40½"	1
Front of seat frame	¾" × 2½" × 40½"	1
Bottom support boards	¾" × 4" × 48"	2
Ribs for back	¾" × 4" × 22"	4
Arms	¾" × 4" × 24"	2
Arm supports	¾" × 4" × 13¾"	2
Swing (oak)		
Seat slats	½" × 1½" × 42"	9
Back slats	½" × 1½" × 43½"	9
Swing (hardware)		
Carriage bolts	¼" × 2"	8
Eye bolts	⅜" × 18"	4
Electrical conduit	1" × 13¾"	4
1" No. 8 sheetrock screws		100
1½" No. 9 sheetrock screws		48
Chain and "S" hooks		

Materials		Quantity
Support stand (yellow pine)		
End A-frame pieces	1½" × 5½" × 72"	4
Gusset for end A-frame	1½" × 9¼" × 22¼"	2
Top beam	1½" × 7¼" × 72"	1
Back brace	1½" × 3½" × 63"	1
Support stand (hardware)		
Carriage bolts	⅜" × 4"	8
Eye screws	⅜" with 1½" ring	2
Machine bolts	⅜" × 10"	4
Washers	⅜"	24

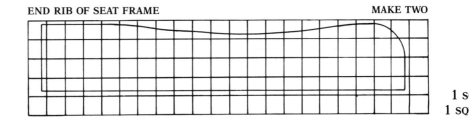

END RIB OF SEAT FRAME **MAKE TWO**

**1 SQUARE =
1 SQUARE INCH**

Illus. 39.1 Pattern for end ribs of seat frame. For full-size pattern, enlarge on a 1" grid.

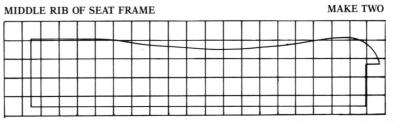

MIDDLE RIB OF SEAT FRAME **MAKE TWO**

Illus. 39.2 Pattern for middle ribs of seat frame. For full-size pattern, enlarge on a 1" grid.

Basic Cutting for the Swing

Enlarge the patterns for the end ribs (Illus. 39.1) and for the middle ribs (Illus. 39.2) of the seat frame to full size. Enlarge the patterns for the end boards of the back (Illus. 39.3) and for the middle rib boards of the back (Illus. 39.4) to full size. Enlarge the patterns for the arms (Illus. 39.5) and for the arm support (Illus. 39.6) to full size. Transfer these patterns to wood, and cut the pieces on a band saw or jigsaw. Sand all marks from the edge of the wood parts.

According to the list of materials, cut pieces for the back and front of the seat frame. Rip material to width on the table saw for the slats. Cut slats for the seat and the back, noting that the back slats are longer than those used for the seat. Cut pieces for the bottom support boards.

Rout around the top edges of the arm pieces using a ¼" rounding-over bit. Rout all four lengthwise edges of each arm support.

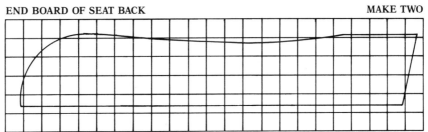

END BOARD OF SEAT BACK **MAKE TWO**

Illus. 39.3 Pattern for end boards of seat back. For full-size pattern, enlarge on a 1" grid.

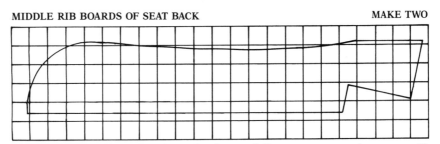

MIDDLE RIB BOARDS OF SEAT BACK **MAKE TWO**

Illus. 39.4 Pattern for middle rib boards of seat back. For full-size pattern, enlarge on a 1" grid.

149

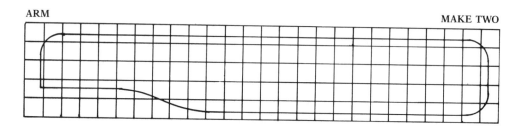

ARM　　　　　　　　　　　　　　　　　　　　**MAKE TWO**

Illus. 39.5　Pattern for arms. For full-size pattern, enlarge on a 1″ grid.

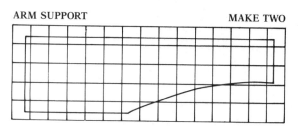

ARM SUPPORT　　　　　　**MAKE TWO**

Illus. 39.6　Pattern for arm support. For full-size pattern, enlarge on a 1″ grid.

Seat Frame Assembly

Drill pilot holes for screws, and secure bottom frame parts for the seat with 1½″ screws (Illus. 39.7). Attach the end and middle boards for the seat back to the bottom frame first with screws, then drill holes for ¼″ carriage bolts. Install the carriage bolts to further secure the back parts to the bottom frame seat assembly (Illus. 39.8).

Attaching Slats to Seat Frame

Mark and drill pilot holes for screws in slats. The slats cut for the back of the seat are longer than those for the front. Mark the screw locations by laying each slat in place and using a ½″ spacer board to assure accurate placement and spacing of the pilot holes. Use the spacer board as each slat is attached to the seat and back with screws. After all the slats have been fastened, sand the ends flush with the seat and back boards.

Arm Assembly

Secure arm supports to the seat end boards with screws. Attach the arms by attaching the back of the arm to the back board by driving screws from the inside through the back board and into the arm. Screws through the top of the arm attach the arm to the arm support.

Illus. 39.7　Seat frame assembly.

Illus. 39.8　End back boards secured to the seat assembly with bolts and screws.

Attach the bottom support boards with screws (Illus. 39.9). Fit pieces of electrical conduit pipe, and drill holes for the 18″ long eye bolts (Illus. 39.10). Install the eye bolts and conduit, and attach lengths of chain with "S" hooks (Illus. 39.11).

Illus. 39.9   Bottom view of arm support assembly, showing 18" bolts fastened through the two bottom support boards.

Illus. 39.10   Arm with eye bolts through electrical conduit for added support.

Illus. 39.11   Slat assembly on seat and back, showing arm support assembly with chain fastened using "S" hooks.

Swing Support Frame Assembly

Cut parts to size and shape (Illus. 39.12). Drill and bolt end parts together with ¼" carriage bolts. Cut parts for connecting the two A-frame supports (Illus. 39.13). Attach the connecting parts to the A-frame supports with bolts. Measure and drill pilot holes for screw eyes, and secure them in place. Attach the chain from the swing to the screw eyes with "S" hooks.

Finishing

The swing and support stand may either be finished in the wood's natural color with just a varnish or polyurethane sealer, or it can be stained or painted. The porch or garden swing pictured was stained with a redwood stain.

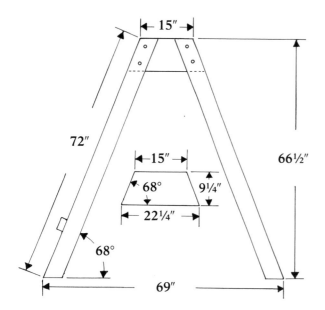

Illus. 39.12   Dimensions for the swing A-frame supports.

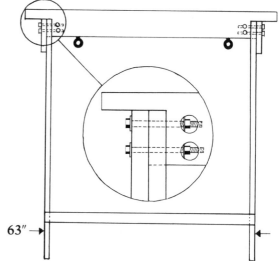

Illus. 39.13   Assembly of swing support frame, showing method of securing connecting top piece to gussets of the A-frame supports.

40 ◆ WALL TOOL STORAGE CABINET

Improve the quality of your work area by keeping your tools handy and organized. The cabinet as pictured shows one possible layout for arranging your tools. You can tailor the arrangement to reflect your tool collection and your interests. On either side of a middle cabinet are two smaller cabinets that can be closed and locked for a compact appearance and convenient storage.

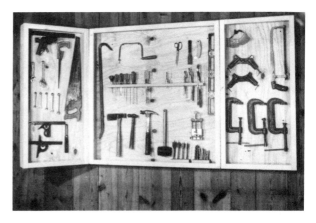

INSTRUCTIONS

The construction features oak plywood sides, back, and doors. Yellow pine is used to face the back cabinet and doors. The middle cabinet is four inches deep, 36″ high, and 43″ wide. The cabinets that serve as doors are half the width, but just as deep.

Basic cutting

Rip ¾″ plywood to width for making the sides and ends of the framework for the tool cabinets. Cut the parts to length (Illus. 40.1). Cut rabbets on the ends of all six of the long side boards as shown.

Materials		Quantity
Plywood frames	¾″ × 3½″ × 42″	6
	¾″ × 3½″ × 20″	4
	¾″ × 3½″ × 41″	2
Plywood backs	⅜″ × 19¼″ × 41¼″	2
	⅜″ × 40¼″ × 41¼″	1
Yellow pine facings	¾″ × 1¼″ × 18¼″	10
	¾″ × 1¼″ × 39⅛″	2
Piano hinge hardware	¾″ × 41″	2

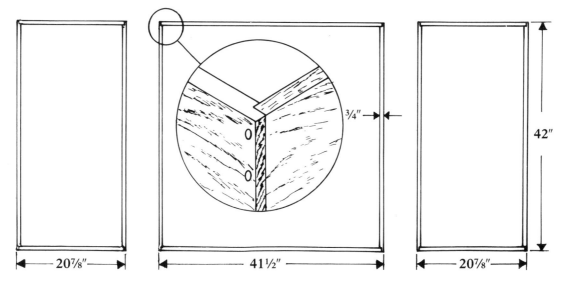

Illus. 40.1   Dimensions for middle cabinet and door cabinet frames, showing rabbets for lap joints.

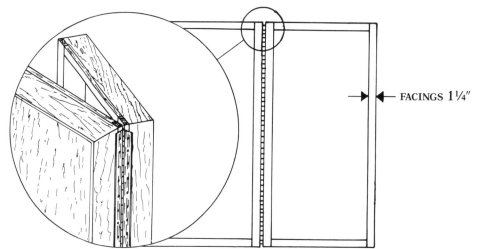

Illus. 40.2 Side cabinet door mounted to middle cabinet with piano hinge, showing detail of view from back side with door cabinet partly closed.

SUPPLIES

- ¼lb. of No. 6 finishing nails
- ¼lb. of No. 4 common nails
- Thirty-six 1¼″ No. 8 screws
- Wood glue
- Table saw or radial-arm saw, with dado blades
- Claw hammer
- No. 2 nail set
- Drill, ⅛″ bit, ⅜″ boring bit, ⅜″ plug cutter
- Framing square
- Paint (optional)

Frame Assembly

Drill pilot holes for screws. Assemble the sides of the frame to the ends with glue and screws. Cut ⅜″ plywood to fit the back side of the assembled frames. Attach the plywood pieces with screws by first securing one side, then using a framing square to square the frame while the remaining sides are secured.

Cutting the Facing Material

Rip materials for making the facings and cut to length. Attach the facings to the front edge of the cabinet with No. 6 finishing nails and glue.

Putting Together the Cabinet

Sand the sides and front of the cabinets. Attach the two smaller side cabinet doors to the

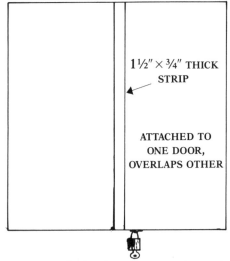

Illus. 40.3 Locked cabinet. A strip down the middle front is attached to one of the door cabinets and serves to lock the other.

middle cabinet with ¾″ wide piano hinges (Illus. 40.2). Attach a latch to one of the door cabinets so that it can be fastened to the middle cabinet from the inside. Fasten a hasp and lock on the other door cabinet. Attach a 1½″ strip to the front edge of the second door cabinet so that it overlaps the door that is fastened on the inside (Illus. 40.3). Both doors are secured with the hasp and lock.

Finishing

The cabinet can be painted or left with a natural finish.

41 ◆ FREESTANDING WORKBENCH

Here is a freestanding workbench that can be used with an existing workshop. This custom-designed workbench does not have to be mounted to the wall, allowing you to work all around the bench. The workbench includes a drawer for storing electric hand tools, a bottom shelf, a wood vise, a metal vise, and removable table stops.

SUPPLIES

- One-hundred 1½" No. 9 sheetrock screws
- Twenty-five No. 6 galvanized nails
- Wood glue
- Table saw or radial-arm saw, with dado blades
- Drill, with ³⁄₁₆" twist drill, ¾" boring bit
- Two metal brackets to fit a two-by-four board
- Two handles for drawer

INSTRUCTIONS

The waist-high work surface is designed for maximum comfort while working on and around the bench (Illus. 41.1), but you should make any adjustments in the height based on your experience with other work areas. The construction proceeds from the ground up by first putting together the legs and the support frame assemblies. The bottom shelf is added and the top of the workbench is installed. Finally, the drawer is mounted, the stops and support board are made and put in place, and the wood and metal vises are attached.

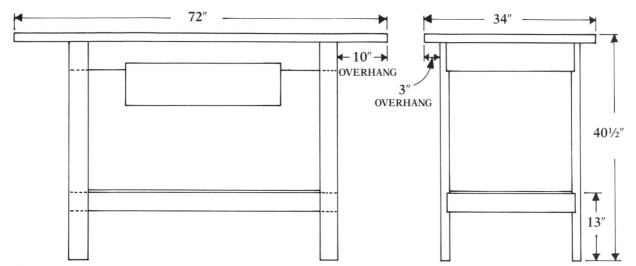

Illus. 41.1   Front and end views of workbench with dimensions.

Materials		Quantity
Fir		
Legs	two-by-four × 39″	4
Lower frame	two-by-four × 52″	2
	two-by-four × 26″	2
Upper frame	two-by-six × 52″	2
	two-by-six × 26″	2
Top	two-by-eight × 72″	5
Support board	two-by-four × 24″	1
Yellow pine		
Drawer box	¾″ × 7½″ × 22½″	2
	¾″ × 7½″ × 27¾″	2
	¾″ × 7½″ × 22½″	2
	¾″ × ¾″ × 23″	2
Drawer front	¾″ × 8″ × 30″	1
Drawer glides	¾″ × 3″ × 23″	4
	⅞″ × 2½″ × 23″	2
Plywood		
Shelf	½″ × 26¼″ × 52″	1
Drawer bottom	¼″ × 22½″ × 27″	1

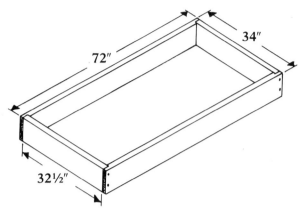

CONSTRUCT UPPER FRAME FROM 2 × 6,
LOWER FRAME FROM 4 × 6 MATERIAL.

Illus. 41.3 Dimensions for upper and lower frame assemblies.

Legs and Support Frame Assemblies

Cut leg boards to length (Illus. 41.2). The legs are notched to hold the upper and lower frame supports securely in place. Using dado blades, cut notches crosswise on the leg boards, as indicated.

Cut parts to length for the top and bottom frames (Illus. 41.3), noting that the upper frame is made from two-by-six material and the lower from two-by-four material. Cut rabbets in the ends of the side pieces for making lap joints with the end pieces. Cut out the middle of one of the side pieces for the upper frame (Illus. 41.4) for mounting the drawer glides. Make drawer glides and wait to trim length until after assembly of the upper frame.

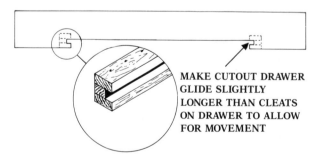

MAKE CUTOUT DRAWER
GLIDE SLIGHTLY
LONGER THAN CLEATS
ON DRAWER TO ALLOW
FOR MOVEMENT

Illus. 41.4 Drawer glides are mounted between the sides of the top frame. Make cutout in upper frame piece.

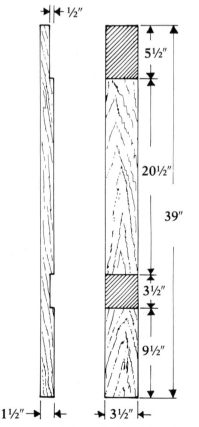

Illus. 41.2 Dimensions for legs showing notches used to hold the upper and lower frames in place.